THE WORLD'S GREATEST MAGIC

Written by Hyla M. Clark
Photographed by Paul Levin

A Tree Communications Edition

Published by Crown Publishers, Inc.

Prepared and produced by Tree Communications, Inc.
250 Park Avenue South, New York, New York.

Publisher: Bruce Michel
Editorial director: Rodney Friedman
Design director: Ronald Gross
Director of photography: Paul Levin
Art director: Rochelle Arthur Lapidus
Editorial assistant: Catherine Cashion
Production: Lucille O'Brien

Printed and bound in Japan.
First printing September, 1976.

Clark, Hyla.
    The world's greatest magic.
    "A Tree Communications edition."
    1. Conjuring.   2. Conjuring.   Biography.   I. Title
GV 1547.C565   793.8   76-19785
ISBN 0-517-52804-5

PREFACE

In the spring of 1974, a short article on magic was produced at Tree Communications. Everyone on the staff enjoyed it, and Ron Gross, the design director, suggested a book on the subject. That was the start of *The World's Greatest Magic*. It was an exciting idea: the task was to convey the mood of a live performance of magic with printed words and photographs.

At first the focus of the book was on tricks and illusions. We planned to feature the individual performers who best presented one of magic's major marvels. We sought the help of Bill Larsen in California, John Salisse in England, and Al Flosso, Irv Tannen, and Tony Spina in New York in organizing the project. Photographer Paul Levin and I attended many magic shows. Our orientation quickly changed. We discovered that the sensation of mystery, the emotional response of the audience to a trick as magical, depended entirely on the performer. Our focus shifted from trick to personality—to the artistry and impact of the individual magician.

We have come to feel that the work of the stars performing in *The World's Greatest Magic* represents the finest magic in the world. However, as many featured in this book were quick to point out, there are thousands of other professional, semiprofessional, and amateur magicians who also present superior magic.

There is no other book quite like *The World's Greatest Magic*. Histories and how-to books abound, but this book is unique in that it is devoted almost exclusively to stars of the present, to the modern performance of magic as a dramatic art. Such a book would not have been possible without the constant help and approval of the magic community. We are deeply grateful.

We would particularly like to thank The Amazing Randi, who guided us throughout the project. He graciously gave us many many hours of his time. Bill Larsen, Milt Larsen, and Jean Kantor of the Magic Castle in Hollywood were enormously helpful in locating magicians for us. We also appreciate the many hours of conversation with Eric Lewis in California and Jay Marshall in Chicago. Mr. Marshall even provided us with a stage so we might photograph Norm Nielsen during a brief visit to the United States. Mr. Marshall also advised us repeatedly and permitted us to reproduce his Houdini posters. We must also thank Emil Loew for making it possible for us to photograph Richard Ross and Flip Hallema during their American tours.

In writing *The World's Greatest Magic*, I have included some of the history of the art so the modern performers do not stand in the void of the present. Anyone who delves into magic's history is indebted to Milbourne Christopher for his fine work and to Walter Gibson for his many books on the subject. Louis Rachow was most kind in making the collection of magic memorabilia of The Players club in New York available to me. Stanley Palm provided additional historical information. Most of the visual historical material in this book is from Mr. Palm's collection, with the exception of the photographs of Richard Cardini loaned by Swan Cardini and those of Channing Pollock provided by Mr. Pollock.

The entire staff of Tree Communications deserves praise for its fine work. Individuals directly connected with *The World's Greatest Magic* were Rochelle Arthur Lapidus, the art director, and her assistants, Patricia Lee and Thom Augusta; Catherine Cashion and Elizabeth Henley, research assistants; and Laurence Barandes, Ruth Forst Michel, and Nancy Naglin in various editorial capacities, and Lucille O'Brien in production.

To the wonderful people who perform within these pages, we can only offer the finished book as a tribute to their artistry. To them and to all magicians, *The World's Greatest Magic* is dedicated.

Hyla M. Clark

Performing in the park on a Sunday afternoon, magician Jeff Sheridan displays the style of the earliest practitioners of the magical arts. It is to such outdoor conjurers that the traditions of magic belong. Like his predecessors, Sheridan is an arresting figure. He is always dressed in black clothing and his movements recall mime performances. Strolling passersby are first intrigued, then enthralled.

The magic of a street player is a community event, a performance that involves both entertainer and onlooker. It is an impromptu drama taking place in the midst of the casual activities of the day.

But street theater is also a professional endeavor. Sheridan has considered himself a professional street magician since 1967. He is quite serious about his work. He is not interested in entertaining indoors. He feels that theater belongs to the street and to the people; he scorns such establishments as nightclubs and theaters. Street magic, he feels, is the truest representation of his art.

THE
WORLD'S
GREATEST
MAGIC

CONTENTS

FOREWORD

When I was first asked to assist in the preparation of this book, I suffered from the usual qualms that accompany such an involvement. Indeed, many of the artists represented in these pages expressed similar reluctance to become involved. At one time or another, most professional conjurers have had reason to regret association with well-meaning persons who have either not represented the Art of Magic properly or who have insisted upon certain inclusions that they are convinced will help sell the book to the masses, to the detriment of artists involved.

Happily, I can declare here that this volume not only meets with my complete approval as a professional magician but achieves as well a new standard for the presentation of my art as pure and joyful entertainment, which is, after all, its primary purpose. As artists, we have never looked better, nor have we ever been better represented in print.

I am very jealous of this pursuit I have chosen. When the charlatans who set out to turn Magic into a racket show up to display their swindles, I am apt to ride off in all directions at once to intercept them. For that reason, you will find that this book insists that those included here be clearly identified as performers of a craft, not possessors of supernatural or divine powers. We are all fakes, but we are not all frauds.

I never cease to wonder at the satisfaction and delight that even after more than 30 years in this business I can still experience after a particularly fortunate performance. My great friend and teacher, Harry Blackstone, remarked to me shortly after we first met that there would come a time in my career when I would feel I'd *arrived*— and I failed altogether to understand his prediction. After all, I *had* arrived! At that time, I was a full-time professional magician working steadily and profitably, and I felt that I had no doubt about my status. Then, at the age of forty-one, after a show wherein I had to meet a particularly tough set of circumstances and had emerged triumphant, I discovered that as of that moment I had become that totally *arrived* magician who could handle any situation in stride. It was a moment of great elation, and surely occurs for most professionals in any field of endeavor. I remembered Harry's prediction, and finally understood it.

Which brings me to mention the often unsung heroes of the trade—the many assistants who constantly leap in and out of boxes and are torn, divided, mutilated, and vanished at the whim of the conjurer.

Audiences very much enjoy the presence of beauty on stage, and I find myself somewhat at a loss to explain why we do not see more female magicians in action instead of their serving principally as assistants. Perhaps some of our readers will remedy this lack for us.

So, on behalf of my fellow magicians in all parts of the world, I heartily welcome you to this front-row view of the wonderful experience of Magic. It has attracted performers of every color, every philosophy, and every nationality all across the globe for countless centuries. And its audience covers the same wide spectrum. We trust that you, too, will become a faithful fan of this ancient art.

We labor long and diligently to attain the skill needed to perform these wonders; all we ask is that suspension of disbelief, which you so kindly grant us. May the rewards of this cooperation continue to be a feeling of delight and astonishment—for all of us.

Populus Vult Decipi: Decipiatur.

Randi

THE WORLD'S GREATEST MAGIC

To stand in the twentieth century and look back on the history of magic is to stand on a winding road which disappears over the horizon, for magic's earliest traditions are lost in the mists of antiquity. Today, magic is theater, a form of entertainment seen close-up across a table or on a great stage with all the trappings of any modern dramatic performance. Although accounts of deceptions as pure entertainment were recorded as early as 4,000 years ago, only recently has the art freed itself from vestiges of the occult. To invoke the muse of magic as dramatic art is also to invoke that of magic as superstition and witchcraft. It is the declared intent of any magician, those of today as well as those of antiquity, to produce the illusion of an impossible, hence supernatural, event. In the eyes of a superstitious audience, a performance of magic might well be considered a display of occult powers rather than a demonstration of dexterity, applied psychology, and mechanical knowledge. A modern-day audience would not likely be troubled by the sudden appearance of golden coins or the disappearance of pretty assistants, but it was not so long ago that even a sleight-of-hand artist was viewed as the possessor of suspicious powers.

The word magic is of ancient origin—its etymology is as distant and obscure as the early history of the art. Philologists and historians generally agree that classical Greek and Roman authors first used the word *magia* in reference to the knowledge and occult practices of the eastern Magi. These Persian magicians were members of an ancient clan noted for their astrological skills, particularly the divination of the birth of Christ. The Greek historian, Herodotus, (484-406 B.C.) gives the earliest detailed account of the Magi. They were one of the original six tribes of the Medes who were eventually conquered by the Persians. Interestingly, the Magi had a hand in their own defeat. Astyages, the last king of the Medes, had an ominous dream concerning the child of his daughter, Mandane. He had married her to a wellborn Persian, Camyses, and dreamt that his kingship was threatened by their forthcoming progeny. He consulted the Magi. The magicians agreed that the child would depose the Median king but advised against the infant's murder. They suggested instead that he be removed to a distant land. When the child, Cyrus, was born they smuggled him away. Upon reaching manhood, however, Cyrus returned and wrested the kingship from his grandfather. The role of the magician was always fraught with peril—Astyages murdered the Magi who had advised permitting the child to live.

Later, the Magi themselves attempted to take control of the Persian empire, but their intrigues were discovered and they were slaughtered in great numbers. The Persians celebrated the slaughter of the magicians annually but continued to venerate the remaining Magi. No religious rite could be performed without them, and rites and rituals surrounded almost every event in Persian daily life.

After the time of Herodotus, the Greek word *magia* developed also into a verb meaning to enchant and was no longer specifically connected with the Magi. When the Roman historian Pliny (23 or 24-79 A.D.) wrote about magic in his *Natural History*, he no longer made a clear distinction between regular magicians and the Magi, although the Magi were known to him.

However, beginnings of the practice of magic occurred in times more ancient. Prehistoric man, scattered over the planet, found the everyday realities of life to be profound and inexplicable mysteries. In his attempt to cope with phenomena he could not explain through his intellect, he conceived of the earth as ruled by a multitude of supernatural beings. Food supply was the single most important consideration to early man in his quest for survival. His focus was nature—the hunt, abundance, and fertility; the earliest divinities in all cultures were connected with the earth. Thomas Bulfinch (in *Bulfinch's Mythology*) writes, "The Greeks, whose imagination was lively, peopled all nature with invisible beings and supposed that every object, from the sun and the seas to the smallest fountain and rivulet, was under the care of some particular divinity." Similarly, the earliest form of worship in ancient China was the worship of the earth—offerings were made to the spirits of grain and agriculture.

In order to deal with the world, humanity set out to converse with these ubiquitous spirits. Primitive man did not separate himself from nature and nature was not differentiated—he conceived a spirit in stone, soil, gems, and metals. In *The Mythology of All Races*, John Ferguson, writing about the early Chinese people says, "There is little distinction between animate and inanimate; all nature is animate." Gold in particular was imbued with power, and precious gems possessed magical properties. Jade and gold were thought to prevent putrefaction; corpses were buried surrounded by the precious substances.

But how was humanity to have access to the spirits dwelling within objects? Obviously, if man is a part of nature, then he must also possess an indwelling spirit. The spirit, or soul, was thought to be released upon death. Ancestor worship followed. In both early Greek and Chinese religions, the departed souls of ancestors were thought to roam above the world, conversant with and able to affect the lives of their descendants.

The next step was the development of a system to make use of these intermediaries to contact the indwelling spirits. Priests were selected whose business it was to cajole favors from indifferent deities, and to appease angry spirits. They were considered capable of accessing the power of the supernatural for human ends. Anthropologists consider the rites of these early priests to be magical, and the first shaman can be considered the first magician. Naturally, such a magician was a man of influence in the community.

The most important province of the early priest-magician was weather control. He was considered to have the power (with the aid of the supernatural forces he was able to invoke) to make the streams flow, the sun rise, the winds blow, and the rains fall. Through his magical efforts the tribe was assured plenitude. His second major function was the control of disease. Early magicians developed practical knowledge of the medicinal properties of plants and some skill in surgery. In a primitive fashion they were the founders of botany and medicine.

The wizard of antiquity had two tasks in keeping his station. He had to develop rites and rituals that would appear to cause the proper effects (failure could mean death), and he had to maintain the confidence of his fellow tribesmen in his magical powers. Naturally, intelligence and common sense played a primary role in knowing when to perform a rite, and a careful cultivation of mystery and presence assisted in maintaining stature.

Dancing, chanting, and rhythmic drumbeats all contributed to establishing a sort of mass trance during the rites which were to invoke the spirits. As the leader, the priest took on a theatrical persona. In *The Origin of Man and of His Superstitions*, Read Carveth suggests that there were skeptics even in the most primitive societies, and very early on it became part of the art of the wizard to sway these resistant minds. It was necessary for him to develop a presentation during which "the power of selective comparison (was) suspended and criticism abolished." In short, the magician, like his modern counterpart on the stage, had to be a good actor. Believing in his vocation would assist this process. But no matter what his personal inclinations, the magician-priest was forced to cultivate mystery. He donned the skins of animals before he incanted and tried to set himself apart from the community. Secret rites of initiation into the priesthood evolved.

E. M. Butler in *The Myth of the Magus* contends that from necessity such magician-priests developed a series of effects which served only as manifestations of their power. Most of these feats—levitations, fire effects, transformations, and apparent invisibility—derived from the earliest rituals, but evolved into performances intended only for purposes of display. Probably sleight of hand and ventriloquism were part of these early repertoires. Illusions of invulnerability (stabbing oneself without producing a wound, walking through fire and the like) were particularly useful.

As communities grew and spread, religion underwent a continual process of development. The indwelling spirits were originally thought to possess a mortality identical with whatever object they inhabited. If a tree was cut down, the spirit within it died. As time progressed, these spirits were thought to use the objects they inhabited as a transitory domicile. The Chinese came to believe that the spirit of a tree could sometimes be seen rushing out in the shape of an animal when the tree was felled. Sometimes rites were performed to entice the spirit out of the tree before cutting it. The tree itself was no longer thought specifically animate, and the spirit living within it became an autonomous supernatural being. Such spirits could move from one place to another, while the objects they possessed lived on with or without their presence. (For example, Zeus summoned the nymphs of the rivers to join him on Olympus without disturbing the flow of water on the earth.) Since they were considered able to reside in different objects, it followed that the spirits were capable of possessing a man. Priests were occasionally said to be inspired by the presence of a spirit, and sometimes the spirit lived within them permanently.

Although civilization became more sophisticated, the single most important field of activity remained the assurance of an abundant harvest and fertility. But the mass of separate spirits was generalized into less numerous individual gods re- each responsible for certain areas of activity. Gods of the harvest or the hunt, for instance, encompassed the spirits in grain or in animals. Local rites and rituals were replaced by great religious festivals honoring these larger divinities. The feast of Dionysus, held every spring in ancient Greece, was a ritualistic enactment of the death and rebirth of the god symbolic of the rhythms of nature. Dancing and chanting continued to be important parts of such festivals, but ritual began to be separated from effect. As human beings became more sure of their place in the world, they no longer considered themselves identical with other forms of nature. By the sixth century B.C. Homer was writing about the lives of human heroes as history, not as legendary tales of spirits. The purpose of magical rites changed, and the idea of entertainment for the sake of entertainment was born.

Gods themselves were anthropomorphized. Occasionally priests attained the stature of deities, and ancestor worship led the way to the worship of the spirits of departed heroes who maintained their human traits. In China and Japan, legendary emperors and empresses were worshipped as divinities. When heroes merged with the gods of nature, hierarchies of deities evolved. These gods had increased influence and although they did not effectively diminish the powers of local spirits, they ruled over larger territories.

The first temples and shrines surrounded the woodland habitats of the indwelling spirits. As supernatural beings were systematized into hierarchies, priests similarly associated themselves with temples and shrines to minister to their gods. Their function remained similar to that of the ancient priests. As agents of the supernatural, they had to provide periodic proof of the gods-in-residence at the temples and their own power to invoke them. It seems safe to assume that some magical techniques displayed by modern wonder workers were also used in ancient days to produce godly voices, divine visitations, and fiery displays.

Temples in Egypt were staffed with several classes of priests. One designation was "master of mysteries." Jannes and Jambes, the magicians of the Pharoah with whom Aaron and Moses contended (Exodus 7. 1-13) were priests of this sort. Neither Pharoah nor his magicians were distressed by the powers manifested by Aaron and Moses as long as Jannes and Jambes could successfully duplicate their demonstrations. Such composure in the face of miracles indicates that the Egyptian court was well versed in techniques of the art of illusion.

Not everyone believed in magical manifestations, however. In *The Illustrated History of Magic*, Milbourne Christopher tells the story of Cyrus of Persia. After conquering Babylonia in 539 B.C., the Persians offered an abundance of gastronomical delights to the Babylonian god Bel as a token of their esteem. When the food disappeared, presumably removed by heavenly hands, Cyrus was convinced of the presence of the deity. But Daniel, the Hebrew prophet, was more skeptical. He had scattered ashes on the floor and showed the king telltale footprints leading to a supposedly solid wall. A cleverly concealed door accounted for the disappearance of the delicacies. In his rage, Cyrus razed the temple.

But even in those early times not all magicians doubled as priests. The Westcar papyrus, believed written in 1700 B.C., some 400 years before the time of Moses and now in the collection of the State Museum of East Berlin, contains an account of a magician named Dedi who entertained King Cheops with marvels. Dedi cut off the head of a fowl which he restored to life, and he caused a lion to follow him docilely. Those who have studied the document concur that Dedi's illusions were presented as theatrical performances and not as occult miracles.

Dedi was lucky to be able to give a command performance, which was not the case with most practitioners of his art. Those who were not using magic to increase their stature in the religious community were usually relegated to the streets where they performed with acrobats, ventriloquists, jugglers, and the like. Such entertainers exhibited their skills at Greek festivals, in crowded Egyptian and oriental marketplaces, and for the amusement of the Roman legions.

Many classic magic effects performed on stage today have their origins in these ancient performances. Effects like the Cups and Balls, the Chinese Linking Rings, and the Indian Basket Trick are all so ancient that there is no evidence of when and where they first appeared. One can only surmise that the Chinese Linking Rings was first done as a pretty trick with finger rings and that the Cups and Balls was probably done with nut shells and stones. The Indian Basket Trick has existed almost as long as baskets. During this trick, an assistant to the magician—or fakir—enters a basket. The fakir covers him with a cloth, pushes him inside, removes the cloth and replaces the lid. With a display of great ferocity, the fakir then pierces the basket with sinister swords, ultimately plunging a spear directly through the center. All this is accompanied by piteous outcries from the supposedly lacerated victim within. Withdrawing the swords and spear, the fakir removes the lid and drapes the basket. He puts his feet in it and sits on the edge. Climbing outside, he waves his hand and the cloth rises. The fakir removes the cloth and the unscathed assistant is revealed. This effect is performed with minor variations (notably the absence of pitiful cries) on many stages today.

Not so with the Indian Rope Trick, which may be the most famous illusion of all time. It has been described thus: the fakir magically causes a rope to rise into the air. His assistant, always a child, then climbs the rope and disappears. The fakir follows, brandishing a great sword. Horrifying pieces of the assistant's body fall to the ground. The fakir then climbs back down and the child mysteriously appears from the crowd. Historians of magic are at a loss to explain these accounts of a trick that apparently was never performed. One theory suggests that the trick was part of a puppet show and not performed live, another attributes the illusion to the fakirs' abilities as hypnotists. At any rate, the Indian Rope Trick remains the mystery of the mysterious art.

Describing oriental feats in the thirteenth century, Marco Polo considered the fakir's displays to be unholy and tainted with demonology. Wonder workers were always dogged by the very success of their illusions. If an effect suggesting a supernatural event was skillfully presented, a credulous audience was likely to assume supernatural assistance—and such assistance was not always associated with good. Even in the earliest times in Greece, people believed in evil demons. It was reasoned that if it was possible to invoke a spirit for good, it was also possible to anger that spirit in which case it would become an evil demon. Demons were also associated with an individual. A nightmare or disturbing vision was thought to be induced by an evil demon. Similarly, a person's good fortune was protected by his resident good demon. In the *Encyclopedia of Religion and Ethics*, A.C. Pearson writes, "Among the crowds of oracle-mongers, diviners, and interpreters of dreams, who swarmed at Athens during the latter part of the fifth century B.C. were some who professed to foretell the future by the agency of familiar spirits obedient to their summons. A notorious instance was Eurycles the ventriloquist who, by giving utterance to his oracles in a feigned voice, persuaded his hearers that they were the pronouncements of a demon lodged within his own breast." Such supernatural entities could also inhabit inanimate objects. Pythagoras (c. 530 B.C) offered the theory that the sound a brass gong made when struck was the voice of the demon trapped inside.

A correlation between magicians and evil can be traced to Persian Magi. The Greeks and Romans believed that Zoroaster, the prophet who reformed the religion of the Magi around 600 B.C., was a black magician. His system included a god of good and a god of evil. Rumors of strange ceremonies performed by the Magi to appease the god of evil associated their name with dread.

Yet, even as today, wonder workers of ancient times were sometimes thought to be divine prophets. The Syrian, Simon Magus (Acts 8: 9-25) was such a magician. The fame of Simon's godlike powers spread so widely and rapidly that the Apostles, hearing he desired to accept Christianity, journeyed to Syria. After being baptized with the Holy Ghost, Simon had the nerve to ask if he might purchase the effect. The Apostles were not pleased. Undaunted, Simon founded his own religion, Gnosticism, an early form of Christianity still practiced today. This confusion of magic and religion continued through the Middle Ages and in-

to the seventeenth century.

After the Christians closed the Roman theaters in the sixth century, the festivals and fairs ended and the entertainers became vagabonds. Conjurers roamed the countryside in the company of musicians, poets, and jugglers. They performed in marketplaces or found shelter for the night at some nobleman's domain. The raggle-taggle wanderers occupied a precarious position. The Church banned all entertainments as profane. It also officially sanctioned the reality of demons. Undoubtedly, medieval conjurers, who had spent so many hours developing their art, entertained no illusions as to the nature of their powers, but much of the population continued to consider them dealers with the devil.

The most prominent magician of the Middle Ages was the legendary Merlin. In contrast to the prevailing attitude, Merlin was nearly always associated with good. Tales of his feats of magic are singularly romantic, and the mood of all the legends is one of lyrical enchantment. It is thought that the original Merlin was a sixth-century Welsh poet who went mad with grief during a battle. Wandering in the woods, he became known for his gifts of prophecy. Geoffrey of Monmouth wrote a Latin poem about him in 1148, and from this story evolved the legendary figure of the magician who used his magic for good at King Arthur's court. The Merlin of these romances was born of a mortal mother (a nun) and a demonic father. His mother, however, repented her sin and Merlin retained his supernatural powers without the stigma of evil. Prophecy was Merlin's forte, although he was well versed in the art of transformation. One of the more spectacular feats attributed to him was removing Stonehenge from Ireland to its present location on Salisbury Plain.

As a mythical personage, Merlin escaped censure. Most medieval magicians were not so lucky. For the most part they did their best to keep out of the public eye. Sometimes a conjurer could attain a protected place in the household of a highly placed person, but more likely he was persecuted.

If the place of magic and the role of magicians in the world were complicated by the entanglement of magic and religion, it was further confused by the intermingling of religion with astrology, and of astrology with alchemy, philosophy, and science. The alchemists were the experimental scientists of the Middle Ages. Most of their experiments were designed to determine whether something was real or not, particularly the authenticity of precious gems or metals. But ancient attitudes had carried over into medieval thinking, and gems and metals were still believed to possess magical properties. Such materials were considered to have occult and natural virtues which caused certain reactions when they were heated, cooled, or combined with other substances. It was presumed that natural virtues could be understood by human intellect; occult virtues could not.

Lynn Thorndike in *A History of Magic and Experimental Science* quotes William of Auvergne, Bishop of Paris from 1228 to 1249, as saying, "Evil ends are often sought by magicians. On the other hand, the apparent marvels are often worked by mere human sleight of hand or other tricks and deceptions of the magicians themselves, but the marvels may be neither human deceit nor the work of an evil spirit. It may be produced by the wonderful occult virtues resident in certain objects of nature." William also believed that magicians could cause the spontaneous generation of frogs and worms by hastening natural processes. Mircea Eliade in *The Forge and the Crucible* offers a similar theory concerning the alchemists. He suggests that in their search to transmute base metals into gold, alchemists desired to supersede time and speed up the processes by which nature created the noble metal.

Some alchemists believed that scientific experiments could not produce a desired result unless the stars were in a certain position; others believed it was impossible to understand a natural mystery without demonic aid gained through incantations. Astrologists predicted the future (at that time astrology was considered an exact science by the Church and exempt from censure), theologians labored to incorporate star systems within religious thinking, and physicians thought evil spirits could be the cause of illness. Often alchemists, making use of the magicians' devices, were considered sorcerers in league with the devil.

The Church was quick to chastise them. Scientists, following in the footsteps of Socrates, Plato, and Pythagoras, were often charged with witchcraft. Two notable examples are the thirteenth-century scientists Roger Bacon and Albertus Magnus.

The names of both scientists became linked with magic, and fantastic tales of their supernatural powers developed. Albertus Magnus was reputed to have made a mechanical man of brass (which supposedly took 30 years to build since every part of the work had to be performed when the stars were in the proper position) that could answer questions. Albertus found it most useful as a domestic servant, but it became so loquacious that one of his pupils, Thomas Aquinas, smashed it to bits. Albertus Magnus also was alleged to have had the power to turn summer to winter and create banquet tables overflowing with delicacies of every imaginable kind.

Similarly, Roger Bacon was said to have put statues in motion and to cause a brazen head to speak. He supposedly attempted to construct a brass wall around England with the brazen head as his link to the devil. Bacon became a legendary hero of almost Faustian proportions during the sixteenth century.

The reality of these two men is quite different from the magical tales which surround them. Both Roger Bacon and Albertus Magnus were reformers in scientific thinking. There are some today who think Bacon was not as original as he claimed, but he is credited with experiments with magnifying glasses, spectacle lenses, and telescopes. Some sources believe he discovered gunpowder independently. At any rate, Bacon believed strongly in the search for truth by means of the experimental method and established principles of scientific measurement. He spent a large portion of his life imprisoned for his alleged magical practices.

Albertus Magnus organized all knowledge available at the end of the twelfth century into a vast encyclopedia. His contribution to the natural sciences is undisputed, but even as late as the end of the last century it was thought that the charges of occult practices leveled against him had some basis in fact. It appears that Albertus, like others of his era, believed in astrology, in demons, and in the efficacy of magical formulas and incantations. However, he took the prevailing Christian attitude that these manifestations were in no way on a plane with divine miracles, and he believed that magical practices should be condemned where any purposeful trafficking with evil was apparent. Nonetheless, he was charged with witchcraft.

In the fifteenth century, the Inquisition began a massive attack on sorcery of all kinds. In fact, the first book containing a section devoted to methods of conjuring, *The Discoverie of Witchcraft* by Reginald Scot (1584), was prompted by the author's revulsion at the inhuman treatment of supposed witches. He exposed conjuring tricks to demonstrate how ordinary they really were, showing that natural events, made to appear supernatural to provide laughter and entertainment, could hardly be considered profane acts. Furthermore, he offered the suggestion that to invoke demons every time something could not be understood was irrational. But more interesting is the list of tricks he included that might have made up a typical conjurer's performance of the day. He described the Cups and Balls, various card and coin manipulations, several handkerchief tricks, a cut and restored rope, a color transformation, and other effects that still provide part of a modern magic performance. The book went into a second and third edition, but toward the end of the century, King James ordered all remaining copies confiscated and burned.

In many countries witchcraft was punishable by death. Inquisitors openly debated whether it was justifiable to promise a witch immunity for confession when there was no intention of granting it. In *The Annals of Conjuring*, Sidney Clarke tells the story of a London magician named Banks and his talented horse, Morocco. This magical quadruped danced, told fortunes, detected chosen cards, correctly divined the amount of change in a spectator's pocket and was even reputed to have climbed to the top of St. Paul's Cathedral. Banks and Morocco were burned alive in Rome in 1608, on charges of practicing witchcraft. However, books on how to perform magic appeared with increasing regularity. Beginning in 1634, several editions of *Hocus-Pocus Junior: the Whole Art of Legerdemain* were published. Undaunted, the witch-hunters contended that those who learned magic from a book were even more evil than those unsuspectingly possessed by devils.

But generally, by the time of the Renaissance, things began to improve for the conjurer. Street magicians who specialized in spectacular stunts received personal recognition. By the seventeenth century stone swallowers like the Italian Francis Battalia, who gulped and regurgitated an assortment of variously sized rocks, and water spouters like the Sicilian Blaise Manfres, and the Frenchman Floram Marchand became famous. Marchand was a human fountain. After swallowing great quantities of fresh water, he spouted streams of wine or beer. At the finish of his performance he sent three giant streams of water upward into the air. Marchand was popular enough to excite general curiosity, and at length a book exposing his secrets was published.

By the beginning of the eighteenth century, magicians were renting rooms in which to display their talents. They would hire space and go about town advertising the forthcoming performance.

In spite of a statute in England, which declared strolling entertainers to be "rogues, vagabonds, and sturdy beggars," promising fines or imprisonment for such unruly conduct, wandering bards, conjurers, and minstrels continued to entertain throughout the countryside. They found the English pleasure fairs, a form of popular entertainment which had existed from the twelfth century, receptive places to display their skills. By the beginning of the seventeenth century, Bartholomew Fair in Smithfield was the most famous fair of this type. People saw Isaac Fawkes exhibit his superior sleight-of-hand work there and watched the marvelous automata built by Christopher Pinchbeck, a London clockmaker. In the second half of the century, Comus excited French audiences with stage experiments of a semiscientific nature. Improved scientific devices—microscopes, magic lanterns, and electricity—were a source of wonderment to the general populace, and conjurers often exhibited such marvels. It was reported that Comus grossed 5,000 pounds during a one-week engagement in London. Eventually, he opened his own theater in Paris.

Later in the eighteenth century the infamous

charlatan Cagliostro appeared. He tried to convince his audiences of his supernatural powers and once pretended to restore a dead child to life. In actual fact, he had substituted a living child for the dead one. Cagliostro was a financial success but his roguery brought him ruin. He eventually died imprisoned in Rome.

In the 1770s Jacob Philadelphia, an American magician performing in Europe, advertised himself as the possessor of occult powers to get publicity. His show contained mathematical tricks, sleight-of-hand effects, and larger illusions. His most famous effect was the appearance of ghostly figures on stage--projected by a magic lantern. The act caught on. In 1794, an entire ghost show opened in Paris.

In the 1780s when the Italian magician Giovanni Giuseppe Pinetti appeared on stage, the classical age of magic began. Pinetti billed himself as the Roman Professor of Mathematics and Natural Philosophy. Sidney Clarke remarks in *The Annals of Conjuring* that Pinetti "must have learnt from Cagliostro the value of ostentatious display." His feats were generally old tricks with new and elaborate staging. He dressed like a monarch, in court attire, and used magic apparatus of gold and silver. He advertised himself by traveling in a sumptuous carriage which rivaled those of the royalty before whom he often performed.

Pinetti had learned the virtues of good publicity, but John Henry Anderson completely outdid him in the early part of the nineteenth century. Anderson had advance men in town before him and entered cities with parades, which were the predecessors of modern circus parades. Like Pinetti, Anderson did not devise original illusions. He used extravagant equipment—gold and silver apparatus—and spent most of what he made on increasingly fancy trappings and advertising.

By Anderson's time, magicians were enjoying greater popularity—presenting sophisticated entertainments at private parties and on elegant stages. Early in the century Bartolomeo Bosco performed before the royalty of many countries and attained lasting fame for his superior presentation of the Cups and Balls. He had learned his skill at sleight of hand while imprisoned in Siberia.

In 1840, Philippe, a French confectioner turned conjurer, built his own theater where he delighted Parisian audiences with marvels employing comic cookery, electricity, and conventional magic. Philippe, who often performed in an Eastern costume, had learned some of his effects from the troupes of oriental conjurers that were beginning to make their appearance in Europe.

Bosco and Philippe, celebrated for their dexterity, mechanical ingenuity, and theatrics, inspired the great Robert-Houdin, the Father of Modern Magic. The autobiography of the French watchmaker, who did not become a professional magician until after he was forty, inspired many other magicians, including the incomparable Houdini. Performing in the mid-nineteenth century, Robert-Houdin dispensed with the cluttered stage and cumbersome apparatus of his contemporaries. He was one of the first magicians to view conjuring as an art form. He emphasized sleight of hand and ingenuity, and manufactured his own illusions and intricate automata. "A conjurer is not a juggler;" he wrote, "he is an actor playing the part of a magician; an artist whose fingers have more need to move with deftness than with speed." He scorned the gaudy performance of other magicians: "This is what may be called the 'false bottom' school of conjuring. Cleverness at this sort of work is of the same order as that of the musician who produces a tune by turning the handle of a barrel organ. Such performers will never merit the title of skilled artist." Robert-Houdin presented his illusions and mechanical devices in a simple setting. He dressed in the formal attire of a gentleman of the day—cravat, vest, and cutaway coat.

In the latter half of the nineteenth century German magician Compars Herrmann, the first of the Herrmann family of conjurers, also abandoned bulky apparatus to perform feats of pure manipulative dexterity on stage. He was the first to perform in Berlin in evening dress, wearing a black velvet suit. Herrmann's effects are legendary for their beauty. For example, he would offer a pear to guests at a dinner table and ask them to mark it in some way. One might poke the pear with a fork, another draw on it with a pen. Herrmann would then cut a section out of the pear and throw it into the air. When he caught it, the pear was whole but still showed the ink mark and holes.

Compars Herrmann was considered the finest magician in the world and Alexander Herrmann, his younger brother by many years, achieved similar distinction. He appeared in court costume, wearing knee breeches, low waistcoat, and court slippers. Like his brother, Alexander was a cosmopolitan man. He spoke seven languages and was at home in virtually every country in which he traveled. Both men received jewels and other costly gifts from kings and princes all over the world.

Alexander Herrmann was particularly famous for his impromptu magic. He would throw a wine bottle into the air at a restaurant and, to the amazement of the waiters, it would disappear. "Such impromptu tricks as these," writes Burlingame in *Herrmann the Magician*, "were Herrmann's delight, and he was endowed with the grace that made him a friend to all men. He was a remarkable raconteur, a continual cigarette smoker, a brilliant conversationalist, and, wherever he might go, a marked personage because of his conspicuous Mephistophelian appearance that, coupled with undoubted abilities as an actor, was of inestimable value in his professional work."

At the Egyptian theatre in London, John Nevil Maskelyne presented a different style of entertainment. He is acknowledged as one of magic's mechanical geniuses and invented many nonmagical devices as well, among them the first pay toilet in England. In the company of such notables as George Cooke, David Devant, and Bautier de Kolta, Maskelyne created astonishing illusions on his London stage. Only magic was performed at the Egyptian Hall.

Maskelyne believed his work to be a true art form. His son's, *Our Magic*, is a treatise on how to present magic artistically. "To produce a magical effect of original conception," he wrote, "is a work of high art...The honors gained by master magicians have been due to a genius for conceiving and fullfilling the requirements of artistic originality." And he stresses, "Now, it cannot be too clearly understood that magic does *not* solely consist in the doing of tricks; nor can it be too often impressed upon the public that the object of a magical performance is not the offering of puzzles for solution."

From the 1890s to the 1930s, the vaudeville stage provided work for a host of conjurers. At about the same time, the great touring road shows came into being. Alexander Herrmann traveled around the world. Okito (Theodore Bamberg) toured the world as an oriental conjurer, and his son Fu Manchu (David Tobias Bamberg) became the foremost illusionist in South America. P. T. Selbit and Horace Goldin amazed audiences on both sides of the Atlantic with their illusion shows. In Brighton in 1911, Goldin presented *The Merry Magician*, a musical comedy starring himself and featuring two massive illusions—the Vanishing Piano and the Disappearing Tiger, but his fans were disappointed—they wanted more magic and less music.

Harry Kellar offered a different show from his principal rival, Herrmann the Great. Herrmann relied on manual dexterity for the greater part of his show, while Kellar presented a performance made up entirely of large-scale illusions. Kellar toured the world with his show. His trademark became the little red devils that peeked out of every poster. As Kellar sat in a chair, reading a sorcerer's book, they sat on his shoulders and turned his pages.

After Herrmann's retirement Kellar was considered the greatest American magician and he, in turn, formally designated Howard Thurston as his successor in 1935. Thurston advertised the event in an elaborate poster depicting Kellar placing a magic scarlet cape on Thurston's shoulders while the little devils looked on. And so the mantle of magic has been passed from generation to generation, from the earliest days of the human race to the great performers who are the stars of this book.

Thurston and several of his contemporaries— Malini, Downs, Leipzig, Chung Ling Soo, Blackstone, Dunninger, and Houdini—together with Dai Vernon, Slydini, Channing Pollock, and Cardini are featured as magicians whose work defines each of the four major areas of magic. With them are 20 of the finest magicians of today whose performances are masterful variations on an ancient theme.

CLOSE-UP CONJURING

Close-up conjuring is a very special branch of the mysterious art. Under the cover of amiable chatter, and seemingly natural movements, the sleight-of-hand artist deludes, deceives, astonishes, and entertains. Close-up magic is differentiated from other forms of the art primarily by the type of props used. Conjuring tricks are small deceptions worked with ordinary objects: coins, salt-and-pepper shakers, playing cards, safety pins, water glasses, or whatever is readily available. Most of the time, close-up magic is the impromptu performance of a dexterous bartender, a magical dinner guest, or a wandering wizard who drops in on an afternoon gathering.

A close-up magician may sit or stand at a table or work surrounded by a crowd. It is necessary that the crowd be a small one, for, as the name implies, close-up conjuring must be viewed near at hand for its subtlety to be appreciated. Ladies are not sliced in half and then miraculously repaired, and assistants do not rise in the air. But the goal of close-up magic is the same as that of all magic: to accomplish an event the viewer considers impossible. Coins may pass effortlessly through a table or change their size and composition. Cards are found where they cannot be. Objects are extracted from invisible purses.

Wandering conjurers of all ages—the prestidigitators who followed the Roman legions, the Greeks who featured sleight of hand at the great religious festivals, and the vagabond magicians of medieval times—are the predecessors of the modern close-up worker. But the street magicians of the Middle Ages, who were known for their unpretentious props and impromptu performances, best show the lineage of today's conjuring tricks.

Many of the traveling minstrels of the Middle Ages were conjurers. Sleight-of-hand performers were often included in the meaning of the word jugglers, and sometimes they sang and danced as well as performed manipulations. In spite of continued suspicion of association with the devil, by the fourteenth century they enjoyed considerable popularity. These itinerent deceivers carried small props with them and displayed their skills on portable folding tables. Sometimes these street magicians would dress in outlandish costumes to attract attention. Hardly men of means, they were often more poorly dressed than the poorest members of their audiences. Many European street magicians wore an apronlike garment with pockets to hold the tools of their trade while they performed. Oriental magicians sometimes preferred a bag hung around their necks. In *The Conjurer,* a famous Hieronymus Bosch painting depicting a presentation of the Cups and Balls trick, the magician has a small basket attached to his belt.

The tricks in the bags, pockets, or baskets of these conjurers were much the same as those which make up a modern performer's basic repertory. Without doubt, the classic sleight-of-hand manipulation is the Cups and Balls. This trick stands as one of the oldest and most widely known effects in magic. The premise is simple: the magician places a ball under one of three cups and moves the cups about on a table while the spectator tries to keep his eye on the cup covering the ball. Of course, whichever cup ought to have the ball under it does not, and whichever cup could not possibly have the ball beneath it invariably does.

In *The Discoverie of Witchcraft*, Reginald Scot mentions manipulators who used bowls or candlesticks with large cupped bases, but the traditional cups are about three inches tall and are thimblelike in shape. A magic wand serves as a reservoir for the balls; the magician produces balls from it and returns them to it at the conclusion of the trick. The props are as simple as the premise, and the prestige of the Cups and Balls is heightened by its very simplicity.

Coins are another standard prop of the close-up conjurer. Coins were first minted in centuries before the birth of Christ, and it is likely that nimble-fingered practitioners of the magical arts began to perfect sleights of hand with them shortly thereafter. Undoubtedly, such pretty tricks involving money would have been useful in the marketplace. In an anonymous work of thirteenth-century England, *The Secrets of the Philosophers*, a section entitled "Deceiving the Senses" describes how to make a silver coin change to copper. (The anonymous author also tells how to make "golden spheres appear flying in the air"—with accompanying directions on how to blow soap bubbles.) Scot mentions several coin sleights in *The Discoverie of Witchcraft* which were standard in 1574. He describes a variation of the Sympathetic Coins, an effect which can be seen at almost every close-up table today. The magician begins this trick with a number of coins in one hand. First, one coin passes to his other hand, then a second and a third until all the coins have moved invisibly from one hand to the other. With equal ease coins are made to fly to one another through the air or through the top of the table.

While cards are the prop most often seen in the hands of a modern close-up worker, card tricks did not make an appearance until long after the Cups and Balls and coin effects. The exact history of playing cards is obscure, but it is generally agreed that in Europe, cards first appeared in Italy in the fourteenth century. The most likely theory is that cards originated in China but were introduced elsewhere in Asia only after their arrival in Europe. It is thought that the earliest Chinese cards were copies of bank notes. There has always been a close connection between gambling and conjuring with cards. Perhaps the oriental gamblers first played games of chance with actual money, then with facsimiles of bills.

One of the earliest records pertaining to cards is an order in 1392 commissioning a French painter to make a deck of cards. Hand-painted, limited-edition props were beyond the means of run-of-the-mill conjurers. It was not until stenciled cards and those made from woodcuts became available in the fifteenth century that cards appeared—and disappeared—in magicians' hands.

Cards caught on quickly. Card games became so popular that by 1526, there was an attempt to banish them from England, and working class people were strictly limited to playing cards only on holidays. But sleight-of-hand artists became unusually fond of cards. A description of a card trick, written in 1541 by physican Gerolamo Cardano (himself a gambler and card enthusiast) sounds remarkably like a model performance: "Thus, this man evaded all our watchful care and surpassed us in cleverness. While he was doing the trick he kept murmuring something constantly as though he were calculating; yet it was certain that what he said did not consist of any reckoning with numbers. But when that well-known friend of ours, after taking a card, looked at it before putting it under a book, Soma said, 'You have confused everything and have spoiled my whole method; nevertheless, the card is the same as the one you drew before, namely the Two of Flowers (clubs),' and we discovered that this was so.

"And although he showed me certain more wonderful things, still indications were that all of them were the work of a certain art of legerdemain rather than of supernatural beings, or in other words, they were much less miraculous. Nevertheless, the art was too wonderful to be understood by human cogitations. And if he had not asked us at various times to draw different cards, I would have suspected that he had substituted a pack consisting of cards of a single kind, namely the 'Two of Flowers.' ...But as I have said, the diversity of the remaining cards precluded that explanation."

Probably the most often seen effect is similar to the one Soma performed, called Card Clairvoyance. This is the pick-a-card-any-card trick in which a member of the audience chooses a card, and the magician correctly tells him what it is. The participant may pick a card from a fan of cards or from the deck. He may remove the card from the deck, then reinsert it, or simply remember the card without touching it. Once the spectator has chosen a card, the magician may handle the deck in an enormous variety of ways. He may shuffle or cut it, spread the deck on the table, count off a number of cards, and so on. Then again, the prestidigitator may not touch the deck at all, giving it to another member of the audience.

Once the card is found, it may be revealed in many ways. It may rise from the pack, appear in a sealed envelope, or be found in the pocket of the unsuspecting participant. Or another member of the audience may divine the chosen card. The magician may even delay identifying the card until he has completed another maneuver, waiting until the spectator has all but forgotten it.

The permutations and combinations of card tricks are inexhaustible. To add glamor, the skillful sleight-of-hand artist executes his personal flourishes. At the conclusion of one effect, he may casually flip the deck from one hand to the other or nonchalantly spread it out face down in a line. With one finger, he may turn the entire pack face up, then face down again, perhaps dallying with it in between. Flourishes are extra added attractions which supplement interludes or finales.

Anything movable is a potential prop for a close-up performer. In the Middle Ages, apples rolled across tables unaided, and wooden crosses turned to the right or the left in answer to spectators' questions. Handkerchiefs have long been useful props. Several coin tricks involving them were practiced in the sixteenth century, and modern conjurers often employ one. A handkerchief can be used to cover an object prior to its disappearance. Sometimes mysterious knots appear which tie or untie of their own accord or can be loosed only by the talented fingers of the magician. Sitting at a dinner table, a magician may use pitchers, silverware, glasses, and even the food itself to amaze his audience. For example, a classic trick is to break open a dinner roll and find a coin inside.

More recently, close-up conjurers have come to use cigarettes in their tricks. A standard close-up cigarette effect is to destroy the cigarette in some way and then put it back together again. Cigarettes may be broken in half or even completely dismantled, or the tobacco removed and the paper crumpled, apparently without damage.

The Cups and Balls effect may be the most prestigious effect in close-up magic, but card tricks are the most romantic. The card manipulator, with his nimble fingers and fast talk, is evocative of the flimflam man, the carnival hawker, the riverboat gambler who effortlessly separate a man from his money. Conjurers legitimize the techniques of the card sharp and the cheat. The magician possesses the manipulative skill to influence the game. But unlike the con man, he uses his knowledge for entertainment only. Certainly, being able to place four aces in any desired location in the pack would be advantageous at the card table; simply knowing where they are would change the odds of the game.

Card sharps can be useful instructors for magicians, since both are professionals well versed in manipulative skills. Robert-Houdin and his teacher, Torrini, both learned card effects from dubious characters. And magicians can help those trying to avoid being gypped. When a conjurer knows manipulations are done, he can observe and reveal fraud at the card table. Master manipulator John Scarne has served as a consultant in gambling establishments all over the world. One of his books, *Scarne on Cards*, contains an exposé of the methods of card cheats. It was written in response to a tour Scarne made of United States army posts as an entertainer during World War II. He was distressed when he realized the number of servicemen being fleeced regularly by professional card sharps and cheats.

Close-up manipulations are more than mere feats of muscular coordination. Dexterity is a major ingredient of a successful close-up effect, but it is not all. If it were, the effect would likely fail as entertainment, even though the skill required thousands of hours of practice.

All magic is a theatrical performance, and close-up work offers a tightly focused view of how all the theatrical elements work. For a coin trick, a card manipulation, or any other sleight-of-hand effect to be successful, it must make sense as a tiny play. It must have a logical plot, build suspense, and reach a satisfactory conclusion. Dexterity is the means by which the effect is accomplished but it alone does not accomplish the magical result. In fact, in the same way that a concert pianist emphasizes interpretation of the score over technique, a skilled close-up artist does his best to conceal the time and effort he has spent in the practice of his art. Like art, magic, does not lie in the mere possession of skill; skill is only the means by which an extraordinary effect is achieved.

Although close-up effects appear to be spontaneous, they are carefully structured events. Generally, the close-up conjurer addresses himself to a particular member of his audience, choosing either one person for his full sequence of tricks or a different person for each effect. He usually begins by asking the designated spectator to do something for him—pick a card or lend a ring, bill, or coin. Already, he has the individual involved and his interest focused on the outcome of events to follow. The rest of the audience becomes involved indirectly by hearing the interchange between magician and participant.

A good magician is a skilled artist and a practicing psychologist. Not only does he know what he will do next, he knows what his audience will do next. In the hands of an expert conjurer, most spectators have tunnel vision. To create the illusion of an impossible event, the magician must conceal the steps needed to accomplish it. He simply does not let the spectators see what he is doing. Instead, he involves them all in following his drama. At each step, the observers try to ascertain what the magician will do next; the magician makes his audience think he is going to do one thing but actually does another. When the magician is successful in his deceit, the members of the audience are certain the ball is under the middle cup or the card on the right is an ace.

The audience is fooled because what it thinks is crucial to the action is really secondary, and what it thinks is secondary is crucial. The magician achieves this deception by misdirecting his audience. His nonstop patter diverts attention from his movements, and his mannerisms are so easy and natural that nothing out of the ordinary seems to be taking place. But each movement has been choreographed in advance to focus attention on whatever the magician desires.

Since the close-up magician is performing in an impromptu situation with his audience clustered around him, his routine must be as flexible as his timing is precise. He must put his audience at ease, intrigue and entertain them. A practiced manipulator can turn aces into jacks, roll coins backward and forward around his fingers, repair crumpled cigarettes. But if he does not also create

theater with his actions and cast a spell, he is not truly a magician.

The bravura performance of a close-up conjurer often retains vestiges of the pitchman and the mountebank. But sleight of hand is equally at home in a well-appointed drawing room or at an elegant dinner party. A goblet of vintage wine can disappear from under a monogrammed linen napkin as readily as a saltshaker from under a paper one, and a diamond ring can appear in a pocket as easily as a quarter. Elegance is as much a part of the tradition of magic as audacity. Since Cheops requested a special performance by Dedi in ancient Egypt, conjurers have amazed royalty and deceived the glamorous. Close-up magic is particularly suited to a small gathering because it can be performed extemporaneously and requires no setup, stage, or special time allotment.

Since such exclusive entertainments are limited to a fortunate few, most people do not have the opportunity to see good close-up conjuring. Until recently, there were few places where a magician who specialized in close-up work could perform. After magic moved onto the theater stage, magicians used close-up effects considered too small for the stage as offstage advertisements. Skilled but little known sleight-of-hand artists gradually gained a circle of admirers among other magicians and friends. Occasionally, they surfaced as entertainers of the wealthy. Today, at entertainment centers like The Magic Castle in Hollywood, California, as well as in bars and restaurants of major cities and convention centers, close-up magicians are at work. Hospitality suites and industrial trade shows offer further job opportunities. But their most loyal audience is still found among other magicians, and their income often comes from teaching their art. Close-up conjuring has wide appeal but it suffers from limited exposure. It is a demanding branch of the art of magic.

A magician creates magic by interweaving his technical skills with his performing talents. He not only creates magic, he is magic. His eyes twinkle. He calls you by name. He makes a small joke. "Blow," he says and your ring appears in his empty hand. "Watch," he says. But no matter how hard you look, you cannot see.

MALINI

Max Malini, who learned to do close-up magic on New York's Bowery around the turn of the century, has been called the last of the mountebanks because he had the impudence of a patent-medicine salesman. Unbelievable in sheer nerve even to his friends, Malini is not much known outside magic circles although he toured the world entertaining the wealthy and the influential. He was an opportunist—the arch-promoter of himself.

Malini didn't much look like the popular conception of a magician. He was neither tall and sparse like Alexander Herrmann, nor leonine like Harry Blackstone. Rather, he was small and squat with very short arms and tiny hands. "From a written description of Malini's physique," writes Dai Vernon, a contemporary master magician, "it would seem that nature had been unkind to him." But nature gives blessings according to her own logic. Malini was always expensively and impeccably dressed, and he had a deep, guttural voice and impressive demeanor. "At first view," Vernon continues, "one might set him down as an opera star or an impresario."

His magic has become a legend. Malini's hands were so small they could not cover a deck of cards; yet his card magic was superb, his timing flawless, his ability to fool even experts undeniable. He could make an entire pack of cards vanish with such finesse they seemed to melt between his diminutive fingers. He built his repertory around his Blindfold Card-Stabbing Trick. Seven or eight members of the audience were asked to choose cards at random from the pack. After these were reinserted and the pack shuffled, Malini would ask a spectator to blindfold him. Then, scrambling the pack facedown on the table, he would borrow a penknife and stab each of the chosen cards in order. Afterward, he might fan a deck facedown and ask a spectator to choose a card. "This is too easy," he would say, then name the card.

Questioned by card expert Charles Miller as to how he accomplished his extraordinary effects, Malini replied, "You don't do it when they are watching...I wait, I wait...I wait until they are not looking." If you imagine a tiny man surrounded and dwarfed by a large crowd of people, this seems impossible. Yet, Malini was capable of completely diverting attention from his movements. "It's in the eye," he said. Through his strong presence, he had the power to turn the attention of the audience wherever he pleased. His name has become a symbol of superb misdirection.

Malini was born in 1873 in Ostrov, a town on the border between Poland and Austria. He emigrated to New York at an early age, and began practicing magic at fifteen, influenced by Professor Seiden, a saloon keeper and magician on New York's Bowery. By twenty he was a saloon entertainer, and soon he had promoted himself to giving private entertainments for the elite. Saloon entertaining remained an important part of Malini's career, but it was in establishments like New York's Waldorf Astoria hotel that he arranged engagements to keep him in fine suits, mellow cigars, and quality whiskey. He stayed for weeks

Malini exhibited three uncut lemons to his audience and asked them to select one. When he cut the chosen lemon in half, he revealed a bank note tucked inside.

and sometimes months at the homes of his wealthy patrons. He was pushy enough to open any door, but he also was sufficiently engaging to delight the very people he bamboozled.

Feats of Card Clairvoyance were Malini's specialty. In this version, he asked six members of the audience to think of different cards. He threw the deck into the air, then caught the selected cards as they fell.

One of Malini's best-known tricks was Blindfold Card-Stabbing. After as many as eight different people had selected cards from a deck, Malini jumbled the pack face down on a table. Blindfolded, he speared the chosen cards with a penknife.

Malini would sometimes prepare a trick hours in advance. There are many stories about how he would secrete things for later use. Once he had made a plan, he would wait all night or all week if necessary to perform a certain trick. If the right time never came, the effect would simply not be done. Malini's Ice Trick is a case in point. Usually

he would work this famous effect at the dinner table. Borrowing a hat from another diner, he would examine it closely and compliment the owner on its stylishness. At some point he would

place the hat on the table. When he lifted it, a block of ice would be revealed. Other magicians knew where Malini kept the ice hidden (he suspended it on a pair of tongs under his coat) and even how he got it under the hat, but no one has ever figured out how he got the ice in the first place. On one occasion, Malini planned to perform the Ice Trick at a bar. The right moment never arose. Naturally, the ice melted. Though his coat and shirt were obviously soaked, Malini continued his conversation unperturbed.

Once Malini was solicited by a wealthy woman to perform at one of her exclusive affairs. He arrived at the train station well dressed, as always, but carrying only a small suitcase. The woman's chauffeur demanded to know where the props were for his show. Malini replied, "I am the show."

SLYDINI

ony Slydini is known in the trade as a magician's magician. A magician's magician does not perform magic so esoteric that only other conjurers can appreciate it. Rather, his presentation so exemplifies the skills of the art that all magicians can learn from watching him. To Slydini, this is as it should be. "My work is teaching," he says. He has been a teacher of magic in New York City since 1947. In addition, he has appeared on televison and performs occasionally in night clubs, but mostly he lectures to groups of magicians and tutors individual pupils. "I have too many students," he says. "I can't take them all."

Slydini's magic highlights the technique of superb misdirection. Not surprisingly, it was the psychology of the art that attracted him in the beginning. Slydini's father was an amateur magician in Italy, and the boy was fascinated by the relationship between the magician and his audience. When his family moved to Argentina, Slydini began to experiment with magic himself. "In Argentina," he says, "I created my own magic. There were many ways to go. I went the right way. I created magic, and it was essentially the same kind as I do now."

There was work for a teen-aged magician in vaudeville in South America for a time, but soon the Depression hit. Even movie houses were having price wars. In 1930, Slydini moved to New York City. "It was hard here, too," he says. "I couldn't speak English. I had a hard time. Finally, I found work in a museum that had just opened on Forty-second Street. After they saw me work, they told me I could stay as long as I liked. Then I found work in carnivals. But I had to start over."

One Christmas, Slydini went to Boston to visit his sister. He saw an agent there while seeking work. "Look," the agent told him, "I haven't got anything, and I don't know your work. All I have is a show at a church for some old folks. I'll give you five bucks for expenses if you want to do it."

"I felt good," says Slydini. "It was something.

Slydini merely slides his fingers along a demolished cigarette to restore it. Try as she may, his viewer can find no subterfuge.

So I went to the church with my suitcase. There was nobody there, not a soul. I went to the dressing room and finally a man came. I asked him when the show started. 'I don't know,' he said. After a while I asked him what time it was. 'I don't know,' he said. He was putting on makeup, so I asked him what the lineup was. 'I don't know,' he said. The church started to fill so I got dressed. I found they put me on second in case I was terrible. But I got a big ovation. Afterward, the man I had tried to talk with came up to me and said, 'What are you doing here?' He asked me to meet him in Boston at one o'clock the following Tuesday. He didn't say why.

Tuesday it snowed. I didn't know whether to go or not. My sister's home was outside of Boston. Finally I decided to go. It was awful weather. I was half an hour late, but he waited for me in the snow. He took me to an agent, RKO. 'This is him,' he said. They gave me a contract for three days in Quincy at 15 dollars a day. I was elated. Then I went to another agent and signed another contract. I worked steadily in Boston for seven years. But I couldn't stay there all my life. 'Hey,' my friends said, 'what are you doing in Boston?' So I went back to New York."

When Slydini started in Boston, close-up magic was not performed as it is today. It wasn't until he attended a magic convention in New Orleans in 1945 that he unveiled his special conjuring. "The world didn't recognize the close-up art then," he says. "No one knew I had this beautiful thing. Even magicians didn't know what it was. When I went to New Orleans, I had a standing ovation for 20 minutes. 'Slydini's magic is different,' they said." Since that time, Slydini has toured the United States and lectured in every country in Europe. "If someone doesn't know me now," he says, "he is not a magician."

The basics of close-up magic, of course, were not new, but Slydini's style was new. Slydini was one of the first to present close-up magic as a self-contained art rather than as an advertisement for bigger effects. In his work there are no lingering vestiges of the pitchman. Slydini's magic is impromptu; he does not have a set sequence of tricks but allows his audience and the situation to determine his program. His courtesy is continental and his soft-spoken patter is charming. He continually understates his case. "I don't like to disturb people," he says. "They don't know what I'm going to ask or how to answer me. So I deal with only one person. I let the rest of the audience relax and experience."

In this gentle aura, the force of Slydini's personality is startling. This quiet man wrests attention so completely that his audience is prevented from discovering how he makes his moves. The Paper Balls Trick demonstrates this process. In this trick, the person working with Slydini cannot see what is going on, but the rest of the audience can. Slydini crumples one piece of paper after another, effortlessly making each one disappear before the participant's eyes. But every time the audience can see him toss the paper ball over the man's head. Eventually, this causes laughter, and the participant looks over his shoulder to see the crumpled papers on the floor. Still, he cannot observe Slydini. "You don't see?" asks the magician. "No," the man replies. "You know why? Because you don't look."

A firm tap on the table is sufficient to allow Slydini to pass a coin through it. The coin drops lightly into his left hand.

Slydini particularly enjoys playing before other magicians. He delights in such a challenge and enjoys fooling his colleagues. "Magicians sit in the front row," he says. "They want to see a trick over and over again." Yet, he is also sensitive to a lay audience. "I do a trick better," he says, "if I like the trick, but if they like it and I don't like it, I will do it for them anyway."

To a master magician like Slydini, magic is a great deal more than just doing tricks. His intricate performances take place on many levels. "You have to know all the details," he says. "Something is happening all the time. You have to understand every moment. You have to know how to hold people, how to entertain them. You must be aware of the common sense of things, the movements of the body, where to look and how to sit or stand."

After watching Slydini pass a coin through a table, restore a torn cigarette, or do some wonder with cards, the audience is breathless. The intelligence of his magic lingers. His work is graceful, precise, and baffling. At first glance, the premise seems simple. Yet, like most things that appear simple, Slydini's magic is deep and complex.

2. In midair, the coin in Slydini's left hand has moved to join the coin in his right. As the trick progresses, Slydini mysteriously passes two more coins through the air until four of them appear in his right hand, much to the delight of his audience.

DAI VERNON

Dai Vernon is a modern Merlin with longish, curling white hair, intense blue eyes, and inevitably, a cigar. He is hailed as an innovator in card magic and is credited with being one of the magicians responsible for establishing close-up conjuring as a branch of the magic arts. He is an impressive man, with fine hands, warmth, and an amiable sense of humor. Articulate and graceful, the depth of his knowledge flavors his words and colors his conversation.

Like many magicians, Vernon started young. He was a child in knickerbockers when he presented his first magic show. "The first show I ever did was in our parish hall," he recalls. "Kids were reciting and people were playing the piano and singing. A girl played the harp; then I did a magic show. I had my patter polished and everything. I was eleven years old. As I walked the three blocks to my house, I felt good. But when I got home, I found my mother crying—I thought she would congratulate me. 'What's the matter?' I asked. 'Oh, I hated tonight,' she said. 'All the other children got up and hemmed and hawed, but you were so beastly professional people will think you've been in the circus.'" He smiles and adds, "Remember, people in show business in those days were looked upon as sinners."

Vernon grew up in Ottawa, Ontario. As a child he met Nate Leipzig, and Max Malini was one of his idols. He attended Asbury College and The Royal Military College of Canada. He was active in sports, captain of the hockey team, and a cricket player. He also gave magic shows, and when he decided to launch his career, he headed for New York City.

When he arrived there in 1913, Vernon was surprised to discover he knew just as much as the experts. Because he was young, he was not always taken seriously. As he tells it, "'Ah,' they said. 'He's just a young Canadian kid who does a few card tricks.'" Once in the city, however, he found plenty of work. Some of the established magicians, Nate Leipzig among them, occasionally were surprised when the little Canadian kid was booked for engagements they might have taken.

(Above) Dai Vernon pauses to display his beautiful set of Cups and Balls. The cups were made especially for him in Iran.

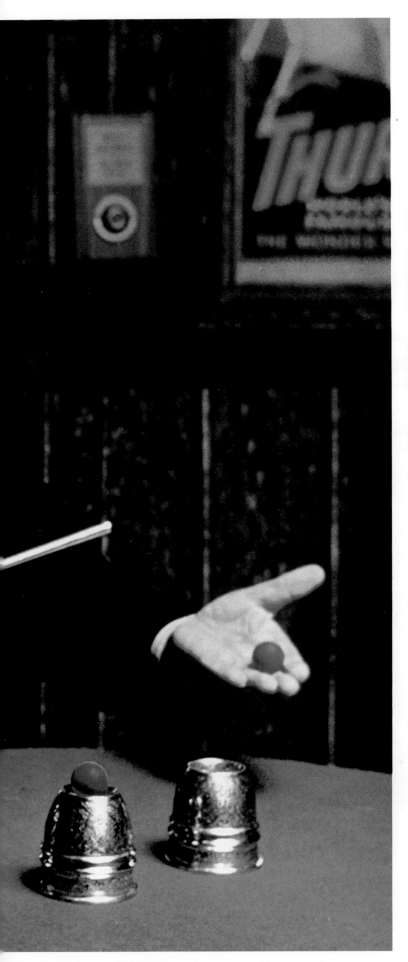

(Left) Vernon produces the balls for the Cups and Balls effect from inside his magic silver wand. The cups as well as the balls have magical properties—the balls appear and vanish; the cups pass miraculously through one another.

Yet work was never crucial for Vernon. Not having money didn't trouble him. He apparently believed it would come to him in due course. "If you chase fame or dollars," he says, "either will avoid you. People ask me how I get publicity. I tell them I try to avoid it. It's not going to do me any good. I can't use it because I'm not in the business. I've never even gone to an agent's office."

Other magicians, talking of Vernon, are bemused. His life itself seems magical. Considered one of the most polished card experts in the United States, Vernon supported himself much of the time by cutting silhouettes in Atlantic City, Miami, Chicago, and Denver. His silhouettes, by the way, are beautifully done.

In Atlantic City, Vernon met a high-society agent, Frances Rockefeller King, who booked acts for private parties. Vernon became one of her favorites. He would go to the parties and if his magic

didn't appeal to the guests, he would cut silhouettes instead. Once she called him in Atlantic City with a job offer and he declined. "I can't go," he told her. "I plan to make money this weekend cutting silhouettes. I go swimming in the morning and have a nice time here at the hotel and on the Boardwalk. I don't want to go into New York." He later found out she wanted him to entertain the Prince of Wales on Long Island. "I've always regretted that," he says. "Life is a funny thing."

There is something golden about a Vernon performance. He makes his art seem natural and effortless. He shuffles a deck of cards in one hand, then casually breaks into a little three-card monte—an old gambling game favored by Mississippi riverboat cardsharps. The cards drop and shift so quickly on the table it is impossible to keep the black one separate from the two reds. In his hands, the Cups and Balls turn to quicksilver. He spins his shining magic wand and a ball disappears inside. When he winds up with large balls, four times the normal size, it never fails to be a startling surprise.

Magic is probably the most important thing in Vernon's life. "If you want to be an artist," he says, "you must devote your life to it. Chess, music, anything. After you get just so high, you realize that if you want to be truly great, you have to give up everything else—you have to dedicate your life to your art." It is the artistry of Vernon's magic that makes the experts rave. He can take a second-rate trick and turn it into a masterpiece. Jay Marshall, conversing about Vernon, describes this ability as perfect editorial judgment. Whatever trick he does becomes his own.

"Some people copy," Vernon says. "They see someone do a trick and they copy. I do my own version. It's no good to copy because when a person creates a thing, no matter how bad it is, it's still his own creation. He will interpret it better than any copier ever could, because someone who copies doesn't know the reasoning, he doesn't know

Vernon flourishes a spectacular Giant Card Fan. First, he shuffles the edges of two groups of cards together, then spreads them out. The cards must be accurately spaced for the fan to maintain stability.

what's behind the effect. He doesn't know what the feeling should be so he doesn't put any feeling into it. That's what there should be in every work of art—feeling."

In the mid-1960s, Vernon left the East Coast for California to visit Jay Ose who had started the Magic Castle in Hollywood with Bill and Milt Larsen. Vernon liked it there so he stayed. Many clever young close-up performers followed him. He accepts few pupils, but magicians want to be

With one card, Vernon begins to roll an entire deck over, first face down, then face up again. He may hesitate in the middle and move the overlapping cards back and forth on their edges.

near him to talk and see him work. His kindness and sincerity draw people as naturally as his artistry demands their respect. Meanwhile, Vernon lives according to habit. He rises late each day and stays up far into the night. He also practices the piano. "For awhile," he says, "I thought I would do an act with a piano. It's very hard to finish a magic act. A dance routine can go into a lot of high kicks and flip-flops, but for a magician it's hard to work out a finish. I thought to myself, 'What a great finish. First I'll do magic and then I'll play the piano.' I still think it is a good idea—a good way to finish a magic act."

ALBERT GOSHMAN

Albert Goshman puts a tape recorder on the table, sits down and places two outsized salt-and-pepper shakers in front of him. "What's your name," he says to the young woman seated on his right. "Nancy," she replies. "Nancy," he says, "I'm going to 'magish' for you." Goshman's 'magishing' is one of the most delightful close-up entertainments in conjuring.

He turns on his tape recorder and pulls out two half-dollars. He holds them in front of Nancy. "Say go," he says. "Gone," he says, before she can get a word out, as he opens his empty hand. He looks meaningfully at the pepper shaker on his right. "Say please." "Please," she says. She picks up the pepper shaker and one of the half-dollars is underneath.

Goshman rolls the half-dollars back and forth across his hands and transforms them into English pence and Japanese yen. He pulls half-dollars from invisible purses and at the close of each manipulation, he glances at the pepper shaker. "Say please." "Please," says Nancy, and every time she picks it up, there is a coin underneath. "My baby blue eyes are irresistible," he says.

(Above) Albert Goshman puts a coin in a young woman's hand and places his own hand on top. But she only thinks she has a coin in her hand—when Goshman lifts his, her hand is empty. (Right) And she only thought Goshman had a coin in his hand.

Goshman's work is an example of a new kind of close-up magic. Instead of performing impromptu tricks in the style of magicians of the past or a series of different effects like most conjurers, he has worked out a routine that is set to a musical score. Using this technique, Goshman can create the sort of unity at a table that would normally be possible only on the stage. He uses the traditional props of the close-up conjurer—salt shakers, water glasses, coins, and so forth—but because his routine is assembled like a small stage show, he is able to use stage techniques. He creates humor, for instance, by repetition. The coin under the pepper shaker becomes a running gag throughout the performance so the hilarity builds. Every time the person on his right picks up the shaker, there is a coin underneath. As a conclusion to the trick, Goshman even manages to place an enormous Japanese coin under the pepper shaker. It is so big that it is visible all around the edges. It is one thing to miss a half-dollar, but quite another to miss seeing that monstrous coin.

The gag continues even when he changes props. He finishes his fast routine with soft sponge balls wildly appearing and disappearing. After a breathless series of effects, one of the red balls turns up squashed under the pepper shaker.

Goshman doesn't look the part of a magician; he is rather heavy with a sort of sad-and-funny face, and slightly random attire. His history as a magician is also atypical. Goshman says he's not quite sure how he came to be a conjurer. But he recollects that he started doing magic one cold winter day in Buffalo, New York. He had traveled to Buffalo from New York City to seek a job at a defense plant. It was bitter cold out and snowing, and he didn't have any money. The defense plant, it turned out, wasn't hiring. In Buffalo he picked up a book of magic tricks and started to practice them to take his mind off his misery.

Magic not only kept Goshman's mind off his misery but eventually made him a successful man. Before he became a professional conjurer, Goshman was a baker in Brooklyn, New York. Friends remember that during his baking days he was always tired, with bags under his eyes, and always lightly dusted with flour. The bakeries required an enormous amount of work and were not a financial success.

1. Goshman takes the coin he has just produced under the pepper shaker and gives it to the man on his left. Making coins appear under the pepper shaker is Goshman's running gag.

Goshman decided to see if he could support his family with magic. Leaving his wife, daughter, and 3 sons in New York, he headed across the country. He dubbed himself "Bakir the Fakir" and tried to earn money lecturing about magic. During this cross-country tour, Goshman learned to identify with his audience. "I would look at them," he says, "and wonder what kind of trouble each of them was having. They became individuals to me instead of just an audience."

Eventually, Goshman arrived in California and Bill and Milt Larsen hired him to work at The Magic Castle in Hollywood. When he began to get other engagements, he sent for his family. He dropped the "Baker the Fakir" title and established Magic by Gosh, Inc., a firm that manufac-

1. Goshman's audience is so overcome by his audacious humor he can manipulate objects without being noticed. Here he simply places an empty glass upside down on the table.

2. As the man holds the half-dollar, Goshman grasps his wrist. He turns to the woman on his right. "Say please," he says. "Please," she responds, already realizing what has happened.

3. As Goshman reveals the coin under the shaker, the woman and the rest of the audience laugh. Then he asks the man to open his hand. To everyone's astonishment, it is empty.

tures magic effects. He travels to magic conventions, lectures on his art to groups of magicians, and operates his business in California.

Goshman's personal experiences flavor his magic. "I do magic," he says, "because I want people to love me." And they do. Every performance has a touch of Goshman's sense of the absurd. He will pull a little box out of his pocket and open it to show that it contains old pop bottle caps. "You were expecting maybe rubies?" he inquires. Bottle caps fly from under his cupped hands to join one another in the manner of the Sympathetic Coins Trick. "Pick a card," he says, extending a fan to a member of the audience. After the chosen card

is reinserted, he pops the deck inside an empty water glass. Next, his tape recorder breaks into mid-eastern music as he throws a small red scarf over the deck in the glass. He waves his thick fingers in the style of a belly dancer, gently aping the levitations of stage performers, and the selected card mysteriously rises under the scarf.

The audience leaves exhausted from laughter. "Thank you," they say as they rise, wiping their eyes. A young boy rushes up to him. Goshman talks to him a few moments as he repacks his little case. "It's the price of fame," he says. "If you offend them, they never forget. You're tired, but still you want to smile." He smiles a bit sadly and hefts his little suitcase in one hand, his tape recorder in the other, and departs.

2. His viewers quickly lose interest in the glass as Goshman teases them with another coin under the pepper shaker. Meanwhile, he slips a huge coin under the glass.

3. When Goshman reveals the coin under the glass, the viewers are thunderstruck. The glass is, after all, transparent. After their initial surprise, they burst once again into laughter.

While a spectator grasps his wrist, Jimmy Grippo splits one silver dollar into two. Researchers at Columbia University clocked the speed of Grippo's hands and found that some of his movements were as fast as 1/1000th of a second.

JIMMY GRIPPO

Although he has entertained the elite around the world, Jimmy Grippo is not well-known outside magic circles. A varied professional life led Grippo to the comfortable position of being magician in residence at Caesar's Palace in Las Vegas. He began working at the hotel when it opened in 1966, entertaining dinner guests in the Bacchanal Room. He wanders from table to table in the public dining room, performing his close-up magic, and he often appears at private functions as well. Celebrities employ Grippo to entertain at exclusive affairs, sometimes having him transported by private jet.

The story of Grippo's life is as improbable as his sleight-of-hand effects. He was born in a small town in Italy. "I was a peasant," he says. "I didn't have any money to buy magic books; so I invented my own techniques." In Italy, Grippo met Alfred Manero, a teacher of self-hypnosis. He became a pupil, following Manero in his rambles through Albania and studying his hypnotic techniques. Grippo insists that he is past 80, attributing his youthful appearance to his skills in self-hypnosis. Manero, he claims, lived to be 118, and Grippo sees no reason why he shouldn't reach 115 himself.

Grippo is a small, dapper, quick-moving man. He dresses well, sporting a stylish black suit, ruffled dress shirt, and the large diamond and ruby ring presented to him by the king of Siam in 1937. He is perfectly relaxed in the elegant surroundings of the Las Vegas hotel. He was equally at ease at parties given by Washington hostess Elsa Maxwell and at the home of President Franklin Roosevelt where, to the delight of the president, Grippo once picked the pocket of FBI chief J. Edgar Hoover.

Grippo came to the United States more than 40 years ago. He lived first in Beacon, New York, some 65 miles from Manhattan. He became involved in boxing and managed the light-heavyweight career of Mario Bettina. Under Grippo's tutelage, Bettina won the world championship and

1. Grippo riffles the deck, offering entertainer Alan King his choice of any card in the pack.

2. While Grippo looks away, King displays the card he has chosen to the rest of the audience.

3. Without touching the deck, Grippo correctly divines the suit and denomination of King's card.

Heat sometimes facilitates magic occurrences. The flame from a pocket lighter causes a coin to vanish.

"I couldn't say no," Grippo laments. "Everywhere I went fat people came up to me and begged me to help them. I didn't have time to help them all. I went to Las Vegas to relax, and the management of the hotel offered me a job."

Whatever Grippo's hypnotic skills may be, they would have to be considerable to match his skills in sleight of hand. Between his facile fingers, a silver dollar suddenly splits in two, and one of the two becomes two again. "It's like a seed," he says. "From one dollar I can make as many as I want." Grippo's audience presses forward as he performs the trick again. Once more the silver dollar becomes two. The collective reaction is almost one of shock—the coin *surely* could not have split!

Grippo's version of the Sympathetic Coins is equally spectacular. Borrowing a spectator's ring, he holds it and three silver dollars in his right hand and three more silver dollars in his left hand. He asks another spectator to grasp each of his wrists. While his wrists are firmly held, the three coins in Grippo's right hand pass to join the three in his left, leaving the ring behind. Then, the ring itself disappears. Producing a sealed envelope from his jacket pocket, Grippo hands it—and the ring inside—to the ring's astonished owner. Grippo passes coins through the table top with equal ease. Instead of dropping into his own hand, however, the coins fall into the hand of a startled member of the audience.

Grippo's specialty is Card Clairvoyance. He will have each of the people seated around a dinner table choose a card, then correctly divine all of them. Grippo riffles the deck in front of his eyes. "I can memorize all the cards in the deck this way," he tells the crowd. "But that's easy," he adds. "This takes skill." He places a selected card in the middle of the deck, turns over the top card to reveal the chosen card, replaces it in the deck, and again turns over the top card to reveal the same card. Wherever he places the selected card in the deck, it always appears on top. Sometimes he asks a member of the audience to pick a card and reinsert it in the deck. Then he gives the pack to another spectator. This second participant then correctly finds the card chosen by the first. Grippo apparently never touched the

held the title for five months. Grippo maintains that self-hypnosis assisted his man in the ring.

Hypnosis, in fact, brought Grippo wider fame than either boxing or his sleight-of-hand artistry. He was given his ring by the king of Siam for hypnotizing him prior to a delicate eye operation. Grippo claims to have been a pioneer in painless childbirth through hypnosis. He has lectured widely on hypnosis, and from the stage, hypnotizes groups of people in the manner of a mentalist. His most successful involvement with hypnosis, however, was at an obesity clinic in Florida. Before moving to Las Vegas, Grippo was associated with a Miami health spa specializing in weight-loss therapy. (Grippo believes taste buds can be deactivated by self-hypnosis.)

1. Entertaining dinner guests at Caesar's Palace in Las Vegas, Grippo offers to drop a silver dollar through a cream pitcher.

2. Seconds after the audience has seen the coin in Grippo's fingers it has vanished entirely.

3. The audience hears a small clink and Grippo lifts the cream pitcher to reveal the silver dollar underneath.

deck. He deals poker hands and the four aces appear wherever he wants them. "But I don't play cards," he says. "It would destroy my powers." A chosen card might appear in a sealed envelope. Or, more traditionally, in the spectator's pocket, or Grippo may cause the selected card to fall through the table into the viewer's own hand. Whatever trick takes place, it is done with dazzling skill.

Grippo is a man of great courtesy and kindness. The hotel staff members speak of him fondly. He is received equally well by the guests who frequent his establishment. Grippo is always optimistic about the future of the human race. He is convinced that the mind is the new frontier, and that by understanding its own consciousness, humankind will be able to achieve the harmony and order

necessary for world peace. Sprinkled in his charming patter are expressions of hope and admonishments against lying or cheating.

"The seed of good is alive in the world. It has always been alive, even if it is hard to see sometimes," he says. "Things always get better. The seed of good will survive." He deals a hand of cards to each of four spectators, then turns over the top card of each pile to reveal their chosen cards. "Oh," he asks in response to a woman's distressed look, "isn't that your card? Here it is, right here," and he draws it from beneath the shoulder of her jacket. "Did you feel it?" demand the others as she blinks, round-eyed. "I felt something," she answers. Meanwhile Grippo is busy dropping a silver dollar through a cream pitcher.

JOHNNY PAUL

The "Amusing and Confusing" Johnny Paul works differently from most close-up conjurers. Humor is a part of every close-up performance, but Paul uses humorous props to complement his comic patter. He is a large, congenial man and his lighthearted entertainment is in harmony with his position as host and director of entertainment at the Showboat in Las Vegas, Nevada. Paul super-

Johnny Paul likes to tease his audience with props as unexpected as his sleight-of-hand feats. Should someone choose the ten of spades, he has an enormous duplicate ready.

vises the other hotel performers, but he also regales guests in the barroom with magical gags.

Paul may borrow a bill from one of the guests and fold it into a tiny packet. When it is unfolded, the bill has mysteriously expanded to five times its original size. "Oh," says Paul, as if startled by this unexpected turn of events. He opens the clasp of an invisible purse and inserts the bill. When he removes it, the bill is only 2 inches long. But what has become of the original money? Paul glances down and there is the bill, on the floor. As the owner reaches for it, the money skitters along the carpet and flies into Paul's hands. His guests are delighted. Next, he might offer somebody a fanned deck of cards. Paul locates the chosen card every time, of course, but while the suit and denomination are correct, the card has been comically altered in some way. For example, an ace of spades may have grown to an enormous size. A spectator who selected the ten of spades begins to crow as Paul draws a card from his pocket. The card he has in his hand apparently is going to be a three. "This isn't your card?" he asks in wonder as he continues to withdraw it. The card turns out to be the ten of spades, all right, but the ten symbols are all in a straight line, and the card is 8 inches long.

Johnny Paul has worked in the entertainment industry since he was a young man in Chicago. He began as a bartender who juggled various bar implements—ice cubes, glasses, beer bottles, and the like—to amuse his customers. Moving from the small bars of the North Side, he first became aware of magicians at the Sherman Hotel. He was intrigued by audience response to sleight-of-hand tricks and enrolled at the National Magic House to study prestidigitation. There he was told to stick to juggling. He was thought to be too clumsy to become a magician—not an encouraging beginning for a man who came to be considered one of the finest card manipulators in the United States. Undaunted, Paul worked on his repertoire of tricks and performed them while tending bar. Eventu-

1. Paul takes the empty clasp of a change purse out of his pocket. Reaching into its invisible interior, he somehow finds a tiny dollar bill tucked inside.

2. Paul seems as startled as his audience by his findings. He is particularly dismayed by the size of the dollar. "This," he remarks ruefully, "is the result of inflation."

ally, he acquired his own cocktail lounge in Illinois, . Behind its bar, Paul was acclaimed for his extraordinary talents at sleight of hand. After ten years, he sold his lounge and bought a supper club in California before moving to Las Vegas in 1963.

Close-up manipulations adapt so well to bar situations that bar magic has become a special branch of the art of illusion. Early close-up workers like Max Malini often entertained when they were customers in a bar, but it wasn't until the 1940s that conjurers began performing tricks while they were tending bar. Johnny Paul, as an originator of this style, opened a new field for the magician. Chicago continues to be a center for bar magic, but such entertainment flourishes around the world.

When Paul touches dollar bills, they have a habit of changing size. Borrowing a bill from a spectator, Paul folds it up. When unfolded the bill has suddenly become ten times larger.

DEREK DINGLE

ists who use one. Dingle prefers this style because it lets him be flexible and mobile. He entertains primarily at trade shows and commercial cocktail parties. "Often one company will hire me to work at a trade-show booth in the daytime, then entertain at a cocktail party that evening," he says. "It's easier to do that kind of work with cards. I don't have to carry any other equipment around with me. I can move freely in the crowd. By having a deck of cards in my pocket, I can introduce my magic unobtrusively; guests can gather around or not, whatever they please."

Dingle considers himself an entertainer, not a magician. He feels that "magician" is a stereotyped word. "When you say magician, people imagine somebody wearing a top hat and tails on a stage, producing rabbits," he says. "I prefer being called a sleight-of-hand artist or a card manipulator. My card says I am a prestidigitator." Dingle feels he has to overcome a certain amount of resistance in most audiences. "Many people think a card manipulator is Uncle Fred doing card tricks at a boring party, where he counts 15 cards and there's your card. I remember a quote from W. Somerset Maugham: 'He said to me, "Do you like card tricks?" I said, "No." He did five.'

"Card tricks have a bad name, but most people have never seen the kind of things I and other good close-up workers are doing today. When people see that you are entertaining them, as well as doing card tricks, they appreciate it."

In his entertaining, Dingle concentrates on humor, not necessarily in the tricks themselves but in his patter. His comic lines are a little spicy. His puns disarm his audience; then he astounds them with stupendous card magic.

Derek Dingle is a slightly different sort of close-up conjurer. Dingle works exclusively with cards, and he is a stand-up performer, using a table only when he is with other sleight-of-hand art-

(Left) Derek Dingle begins each performance by introducing himself to his audience. "It's my real name," he tells them.

(Opposite) "Well, Barbara," says Dingle, addressing the woman in front of him, "would you like to pick a card then?"

"What's your name?" he asks, extending a card to a young woman. "Judy," she answers. "Judy, I'd like to lay you ten to one odds that I'm going to find your card." She draws a card. He holds the deck behind his back. "I'll do it in the dark," he says, closing his eyes. He takes three cards from the deck and offers them to her. "Point to your card." She indicates the middle card. But he has been turning the cards in his hands and he shows her the top card. It is her card. "Ah," he says, "but you picked the middle card." He shows her the middle card, and it is her card, too. He keeps turning the cards in his hands, and every card is her card. "You think all of these cards are the same, don't you?" he asks. "But none of them have faces." He spins them over and on top of each other, and they are the same on both sides. The numbers have magically disappeared. "And really, none of them is your card." He turns them over and of the three cards, none is hers. "You've only got two eyes," he says, "and I talk a lot."

Dingle's history with magic, as well as his skill, is unusual in the profession. Like many magicians, he started with a magic set as a child. He played with magic, but unlike most practitioners of the art, he dropped the hobby by his mid-teens. Years later, when he moved from England to Canada, Dingle became involved in conjuring when he met Ross Bertram, a virtuoso of close-up magic. An even greater influence was Eddie Fechter, a bar owner and magician in Buffalo, New York. "I used to drive down there from Toronto twice a week just to see him," Dingle recalls. "I practiced eight hours a day on card tricks."

Dingle spent four years in Canada, then moved to New Jersey where he lives, not far from New York City. But it wasn't until 1974 that he became a professional conjurer, and other magicians are amazed that he is so polished after such a short time in the field. "It all actually started when my boss called me into his office and said, 'You're fired.' I thought that was a good time to quit," he says. "I used to do magic as a hobby but I decided if I was going to get invited to parties to do card tricks, I might as well earn a living that way." Indeed, Dingle makes a good living with his magic.

He appears at trade shows and private parties and says he does as well as when he was an engineer. He was, incidentally, a successful engineer.

Dingle does not confine his effects to one member of the audience when he performs. He moves from one person to another with each manipulation. "If I can pick out a good reactor," he says, "the rest of the audience will enjoy the reaction. If I interact well with a person and he throws me lines, the rest of the audience enjoy it. That's why it's so hard to do close-up magic on television. One tends to be just a pair of hands. The camera comes in close, and it cuts me out as a personality. So I can get no reaction from the audience. No lines. That's very tough because close-up magic is such a personal thing. Television is a good medium because

As Dingle works, he talks to various members of his audience. Here he challenges a gentleman who has chosen a card. "I'll bet you think none of these cards is yours," he says.

44

otherwise close-up magic is seen by so few people, but it's very hard. If you have an overall picture, no one can see the cards. If you zoom in on the cards, you don't see the overall framework, and you miss the reactions."

Reaction to Dingle's tricks from a lay audience is laughter; from other magicians, it is respect for his work. Within the profession Dingle is known as a modern innovator. "There are not many people in magic who are innovators as well as performers," he says. "Most do other people's routines. To create your own routine, you use a basic set of moves and develop them just like you use the notes on a piano to make a tune. But you can't be an instant magician. So many people think anyone can be a magician. They walk into a magic store and buy a box and go out to annoy their friends with it. Because it's the nature of magic to fool people, a bad magician sometimes comes off as well as a really good one. A lay audience can't always appreciate the art of magic. People think I have a trick deck or something. But there's no way I could do the things I do with a trick deck of cards."

Whether or not a lay audience can appreciate the finer points of Dingle's magic, it certainly can appreciate his performance. "I never knew a magician could be like that," said one woman after watching him. "How does he do it?" Says Dingle, "If you really believed your eyes, you wouldn't be standing there, you'd be kneeling."

His audience looks in his hands for the chosen ace of spades, but Dingle has stuck the card to his forehead. One by one, the watchers discover their mistake, pointing and laughing.

Dingle apparently cannot find the chosen card. But just as the spectator starts to become overconfident, the selected ace of diamonds suddenly materializes in Dingle's hands.

STAGE AND CABARET MAGIC

As in close-up conjuring, cabaret and stage effects are differentiated from other branches of the magical arts by the kinds of props used. A cabaret or nightclub effect (usually, but not always, performed on stage) uses props small enough to be carried in a suitcase. In general, these effects can be performed in the round with the audience on all sides of the performer. But a cabaret effect is large enough to be seen at some distance so it also can be presented in a theater of average size.

Cabaret magic shares the same heritage as close-up conjuring, but the style of performance has been different from the start. Predecessors of the modern stage magician were Greek fire-eaters who performed at fairs around 300 B.C., Indian fakirs who materialized cobras in equally distant times, and Europe's stone swallowers and water spouters of the Middle Ages. They were all street workers like the sleight-of-hand artists and specialized in impromptu entertainments performed in the midst of a crowd for whatever money would be tossed to them.

Little is new in magic, and most of the effects now seen in nightclubs and theaters have their roots in deceptions of antiquity. The Needle Trick, for example, in which a magician appears to swallow needles and thread, then produces lengths of threaded needles from his mouth is as ancient as the Cups and Balls effect. It was first performed centuries ago with beads and horsehair in the crowded streets of the Orient.

In 1700 B.C., the Egyptian magician Dedi performed the first decapitation effect when he cut off the head of a fowl and restored it to life. In the Middle Ages, magicians substituted a human being for the bird and called it the John the Baptist illusion. Since the earliest shaman proved his invulnerability by appearing to stab himself, street performers have delighted in pretended lacerations. In *Hocus-Pocus: The Whole Art of Legerdemain*, written in 1622, there are numerous descriptions of how to create effects of this sort—cutting off one's nose or thrusting a needle into the forehead. Such effects are rarely part of a modern stage performance but are still seen in carnival side shows.

Jugglers, sword-swallowers, fire-eaters, and other conjurers often worked with street merchants to help them hawk their wares. The performers first drew the crowds; then the salesman made his pitch.

In a discussion of street theater in *Popular Entertainments Through the Ages*, Samuel McKechnie quotes a sixteenth-century description of one enterprising seller: "Also I have seen a mountebank hackle and gash his naked arm with a knife most pitifully to beholde, so that the blood hath streamed out in great abundance, and by and by after he hath applied a certain oyle unto it, wherewith he hath incontinently both stanched the blood and so thoroughly healed the woundes and gashes, that when he hath afterward shewed us his arme againe, we could not possibly perceive the least token of a gash." Customer satisfaction guaranteed.

The classic cabaret effect is also one of the oldest. There are few feats as breathtaking as a skilled presentation of the Chinese Linking Rings. Like the Cups and Balls, the elegant simplicity of the props and premise intensifies the mystery and beauty of the effect. In its modern manifestations, the rings are made of highly polished steel eight inches in diameter. The magician may work with any number of rings from four to ten or eleven. The performer displays one of an almost endless number of variations on the same theme. The premise is uncomplicated: solid steel rings are made to pass through one another as easily as if they were of some ethereal substance. A member of the audience will find it impossible to separate the linked rings, but the magician, master of mysteries, lifts them and they fall apart.

When the Linking Rings was first performed is a fact lost in time. It is surmised that the trick was first practiced with finger rings and gradually evolved into its present form. In France, Philippe became one of the first occidental performers to present the Linking Rings during the first half of the nineteenth century. He had witnessed a performance by oriental mystics in London from whom he learned the secret of the rings, as well as another traditional Chinese standard—the appearance of a goldfish bowl full of fish and water. Philippe, dressed in fanciful oriental attire, stood on a small platform. He displayed a spangled shawl and exhibited both sides to the audience. He threw the shawl down, then lifted it to reveal the goldfish bowl. He produced a second and third bowl in this manner and then similarly populated the platform with chickens, ducks, and rabbits.

Magic owes much to oriental practitioners. Some other cabaret effects of eastern origin belong to a genre called botanical magic. In the manner of Aaron's blessed rod, bare trees were made to flower spontaneously and produce fruit. Brahman priests of India mentioned magic of this sort in writings dating from the first century, but effects of this kind were not presented by an occidental conjurer until Robert-Houdin introduced a spectacular fruit-producing orange tree on the Parisian stage in the 1840s. Spontaneous flower productions, together with blooming trees of all varieties, became a favorite during the classical age of magic in the nineteenth century. But in general, such effects have fallen out of favor on the modern stage.

The type of trick currently seen most often is known as a production in which objects, one after another, materialize out of thin air in the magician's fingers. There are card, coin, cigarette (lit and unlit), dove, parakeet, and billiard ball productions, as well as almost every other kind of production imaginable.

The classic coin production titled The Miser's Dream has long been a favorite among magicians. Reginald Scot describes an early version of the trick in *The Discoverie of Witchcraft* (1584). In the standard version, the prestidigitator produces first one coin, then another, and still more at an increasingly rapid rate until golden coins are dripping from his hands.

There are also many forms of multiplication. In a multiplication, one object suddenly doubles, then quadruples. The magician holds up one billiard ball, spreads his fingers and has four. He raises his hands with a thimble on each index finger, turns them and immediately has one on every finger of both hands.

Silks have become a magic tradition and are nearly always used in cabaret effects, either alone or in combination with other articles. They make an ideal prop, not only because of their decorative value but because they are highly visual and not in any way unnatural. Silks may change color before the eyes, seem to increase in number with the flick of the wrist or pop out of a pocket.

Since the demise of the ostentatious stage presentations of the early nineteenth century, magicians have tended to avoid equipment that seems odd. Thimbles, cards, coins, billiard balls, and scarves are all items that are visual but not startling. The reliance of the modern stage magicians on such props is a departure from their forerunners in the street and on stage. Medieval magicians, borrowing from the alchemists, often billed themselves as professors or philosophers. In keeping with the dignity of their self-assumed titles, they used apparatus vaguely scientific and termed their effects natural wonders. One of the more famous of these street magicians was Doctor Katterfelto who performed with a black cat in London in the 1780s. He intimated that he was of Prussian descent, the son of an influential family, and although he was a charlatan, he evidenced some education and wit. Katterfelto termed himself a Divine and Moral Philosopher and exhibited in his show of *Wonderful Wonders* a microscope which made it possible to see hundreds of insects in a drop of milk, water, or vinegar. Katterfelto made much of his cat's abilities and led his audience to believe she possessed extraordinary powers of her own. Although eccentric, Katterfelto was typical of the magicians of the time. He would hire a room at an inn, pass out handbills advertising his performances, and affect the garb of a scholar—a long robe and square hat. While presenting his microscope and other wonders, he would lecture on science and philosophy.

On the street, a magician like Doctor Katterfelto did not have to project himself or his tricks for any distance. He captured his audience in the same manner as an exhibitor of a medicine show. Usually anonymous and itinerant, the street magician was little concerned with manipulating a large audience.

But once the conjurer stepped on stage, he was subject to many new constraints. To entertain those at the back of the theater, the performer had to heighten the impact of his effects and his own personality. At about the same time that Doctor Katterfelto was working on the streets of London, Giuseppe Pinetti first moved into a Paris theater. While sleight-of-hand artists of superior talents lived in poverty and performed for pennies, Pinetti gambled for money and fame. The larger audience in a theater meant increased profits. Pinetti succeeded not so much because of his talents of legerdemain but because he understood the art of showmanship.

On stage, Pinetti performed the standard illusions of his day: the Decapitation, the Beads on a String, the Egg Bag. (The Egg Bag, invented in the seventeenth century and most popular during the eighteenth, involved placing an egg inside a black bag, vehemently crushing the bag, and finally removing an unbroken egg.) He made omelettes in his hat and exhibited mechanical men—a Wise Little Turk and a Grand Sultan correctly answered questions put to them by members of the audience. Pinetti solved the demands of expanded space not with new effects but with creative staging. When he opened in Paris in 1780, Pinetti wore the dress of the French court. Attired in satin pants, brocade coat, silk stockings, and powdered wig, he performed in an elegant drawing room setting. He changed his costumes two or three times during each performance. His mannerisms befitted his appearance, and his apparatus was silver and gold. He was invited to perform for Louis XVI and later gave other command performances on tour in England, Russia, and Germany.

Pinetti discovered the advantages of stardom and recognized the need for an effective offstage personality. In keeping with his regal demeanor, he drove an impressive coach. While sipping afternoon tea, he extracted coins from cakes. As he wandered through local shops, he practiced small tricks for shopkeepers and patrons—exciting their interest in his forthcoming show.

Although Pinetti was among the first to present magic on stage, his style was too archaic for him to qualify as a modern magician. The title of The Father of Modern Magic belongs to Robert-Houdin, who heralded the current age of magic in nineteenth-century France. Robert-Houdin dispensed with the outlandish stage settings and affected attire and concentrated instead on effective presentation. He revolutionized the nature of wizardry by his conception of the magician as an actor and an artist rather than a personality or a rogue. His autobiography is the story of the romance of a man with magic. He delights in his inventions, stresses the need for constant practice, and always speaks on the dramatic rapport necessary between the magician and his audience.

Although the modern stage or cabaret magician is working in a different environment, he must accomplish the same result as a close-up conjurer. He, too, must draw the audience into the suspense of the action on stage and surprise viewers with unexpected results. His medium is different, but the fundamentals of his performance remain substantially the same.

On the stage, a magician must create an act with dramatic unity. Each effect must blend with the performance as a whole to sustain suspense, maintain continuity, and reach a climactic conclusion. To accomplish this, the magician must relate his effects to one another. Usually, he develops a theme based on the nature of his props, or he creates a character and relies on its dramatic personality to maintain cohesion.

If a magician uses character as the basis for his act, the personality he assumes is usually, but not always, that of a magician. The magician can be himself in the role of a magician while on stage, or can impersonate a fictionalized conjurer or other character. Famous stage magicians like Robert-Houdin, Compars Herrmann, and Alexander

Herrmann expanded their own personalities on stage. In fact, they are responsible for the image most people have when they hear the word magician. Robert-Houdin was among the first to perform in the evening dress that became traditional, and Compars Herrmann provided the rest of the standard costume: silk hat, cape, and small goatee. Alexander Herrmann never relinquished his magician's image, even offstage. He delighted in spontaneous conjuring, even performing such feats as producing his cab fare from the air.

In the late nineteenth and early twentieth centuries, the American William Ellsworth Robinson assumed the character of a magician other than himself and became a Chinese wizard, Chung Ling Soo. He based his act on oriental effects, wore oriental attire, and even became Chinese offstage. Oriental roles became quite as popular as the more standard wizard in evening dress. However, it is not essential for a magician to act like a magician on stage. He may become a pool hustler with magical cue and balls, a tramp, a *commedia dell'arte* figure, or even a clown.

Props also assure the continuity of a performance, as in the case of the Fire Kings and Fireproof Men popular in the nineteenth century. Singularly bizarre in his approach, Ivan Ivanitz Chabert swallowed acids, boiling oil, and molten lead in the 1850s. At the end of his act, he climbed inside an oven where he simultaneously roasted a piece of meat. After he emerged uncharred, he invited a member of the audience on stage to share his meal. More often, however, routines are constructed around coins, cards, scarves, or birds. Harry Houdini, for example, was once the King of Cards.

Most modern cabaret acts and stage sequences are short and silent. In part, this is a result of the short time allotted acts during the vaudeville era from the 1890s to the 1930s. In the nineteenth century during the classical age of magic, magicians like Philippe, Robert-Houdin, and John Henry Anderson performed in their own theaters where their programs lasted several hours. Most performers, however, found such ventures prohibitively expensive. By the end of the century, street players were passing out of vogue. Conjurers performed instead in music hall variety shows and tap room concerts. These entertainments had developed out of the strolling minstrels' attempt to circumvent the legitimate theater in the seventeenth and eighteenth centuries, and they in turn spawned vaudeville. In the latter part of the nineteenth century men like Tony Pastor moved vaudeville out of the beer halls and made it family entertainment. By the early twentieth century great chains of vaudeville houses dominated the field. In most houses, songs and jokes and other specialties were presented from 10 A.M. until 11 P.M. No longer having an entire afternoon at his disposal, the magician had to compress his act. He became mute, because a silent conjurer can perform many more effects than one who talks. Silent acts also met the ever-present need to develop routines with international appeal.

Working in silence and at a distance, the stage magician must reach his audience through pantomime. Cabaret effects depend more upon choreography than plot. The actions that accomplish the effects are concealed within the dance movements. Even the parts of the standard stage costume have their uses. The magician enters the stage and bows. He removes his top hat and places it on a small table. Almost immediately, his cane disappears and his white gloves turn to doves. The hat becomes an obvious receptacle for the cards he pulls from the air. The magician maps a direction for his actions so the end of one sequence logically flows into the next. If the rhythm and timing of the performance are lost, effects become disjointed in a way that detracts from the dramatic intensity of the entire performance. Music is an effective aid, and many magicians either provide their own or work with the musicians present at most variety shows.

A successful magician performing cabaret effects presents a routine with sufficient impact, visually and emotionally, that invites the audience to join with him in the fantasy he creates. Like the close-up conjurer, a skilled cabaret magician is an artist. He makes his audience care about what he is doing—care about his silks, his birds, and himself. Bright coins pour from his hands, metal becomes permeable, doves turn to silks. A skilled magician stirs the imagination as he pleases the mind.

NATE LEIPZIG AND T. NELSON DOWNS

Nate Leipzig astounded both magicians and lay audiences with his deft card manipulations on the vaudeville stage.

T. Nelson Downs, shown above in an unaccustomed moment of repose, concentrated on coin magic.

After vaudeville moved out of beer halls and became respectable entertainment, it offered work for thousands of magicians. Outstanding among them are two pioneer names: Nate Leipzig and T. Nelson Downs.

Nate Leipzig was born in Sweden in 1873. Although he was to become a conjurer of world renown, he made his name in American vaudeville. While he was completely at home with an array of small effects, Leipzig built his reputation on superior card manipulations. His most famous trick was called Slapping the Aces. Leipzig would ask four

people to insert the four aces into a deck of cards. Then, simply by slapping the top card, he would change it to each of the aces in succession.

Leipzig performed most often in the homes of the wealthy and at the Lamb's Club bar in New York City. When he brought his work to the vaudeville stage, his performance was a cross between the close-up worker and the stage magician. He did not perform in the intimate style of the modern close-up magician with a crowd clustered all around him but from the stage of a small theater where he was able to entertain audiences of up to 600 people. He would invite a few members of the audience to join him on stage as he performed card tricks and coin manipulations. They were a representative audience on stage through whom he could reach the rest of the house. When movies became popular, films of Leipzig's hands were shown while he worked.

Magicians were entranced by the beauty of his work. His skill was so natural he seemed not to be aware of the complexity of what he was doing. He performed as easily as he breathed, as if perform-

theater himself. By the end of the century, Downs was receiving one of the largest salaries in American vaudeville.

Vaudeville acts were rarely more than ten minutes long. To stand out among the many short bits, performers often developed specialty acts—novelties to attract attention. Downs dubbed himself the King of Koins and confined himself to working with only one kind of prop. His methods were often original; he was the first sleight-of-

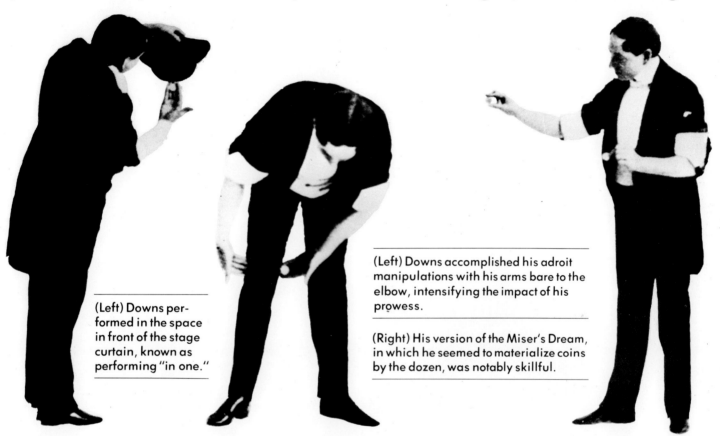

(Left) Downs performed in the space in front of the stage curtain, known as performing "in one."

(Left) Downs accomplished his adroit manipulations with his arms bare to the elbow, intensifying the impact of his prowess.

(Right) His version of the Miser's Dream, in which he seemed to materialize coins by the dozen, was notably skillful.

ing required no effort at all. He was called the Paderewski of card manipulators because he played with cards like the great pianist played on the keyboard. "Nate neither juggled nor manipulated," writes Fred Keating in an article in *Sphinx* magazine. "He caressed (the cards), he whispered to them, he enchanted them and thereby drew from them mystery, drama—never card tricks."

T. Nelson Downs was as proficient with coins as Leipzig was with cards. Born in Iowa in 1876, Downs decided to try his luck on stage after practicing coin manipulations while working as a railroad ticket agent. Downs first broke into vaudeville on the London stage, and his rapid success there prompted Howard Thurston to try English

hand artist to perfect the continuous movement of a coin from the back to the front of the hand.

Downs was a good looking, sandy haired, clean shaven man with a fine stage presence and an affable manner. His version of the Miser's Dream was spectacular. According to Professor Hoffman in *Modern Magic*, "...(W)ith the Midas touch (he) minted groats and guineas and pieces of silver at his twinkling fingertips."

Although Downs was lauded for his expertise, magicians ruefully commented that the specialization he made popular nearly undermined the art. Soon stages were flooded with coin, card, and cigarette manipulators—and most of them had nowhere near the skill of their model.

Swan and Richard Cardini are pictured at Chicago's Palmer House Hotel. Cardini always dressed in full formal attire. Swan, in her page's costume, was often mistaken for a young boy.

CARDINI

Richard Cardini is credited with numerous achievements in the field of magic. An innovative manipulator, he was the first magician to make card fans and lighted cigarettes materialize. He liked to tinker with intricate mechanical devices and built many effects for other magicians as well as himself. But his most noteworthy accomplishments were his beautiful performances. "When I'm working," he said, "I try to convey the impression that I'm not doing conjuring tricks." He was successful: magicians and reviewers alike commented on the artistry of Cardini's routines.

Cardini was born Richard V. Pitchford in a small Welsh fishing village in 1894. Pitchford's family was not wealthy, and he began working in the local packing house and as a bellboy at an early age. Like many children, he experimented with conjuring tricks. At seventeen, Pitchford enlisted in the British army. During his army days it occurred to him to take his abilities at sleight of hand seriously. He perfected his production of card fans in the trenches of World War I. Because it was cold on the battlefield, Pitchford found it necessary to practice while wearing gloves. It was hard to produce single cards under those conditions so he often made them materialize in clumps instead. One British officer, a Lieutenant Legge, remarked that he had never seen a magician produce fans of cards. Pitchford recognized the novelty of his effect and began working on the conscious production of card fans. Legge was destined to play another role in Pitchford's career. He was the model for Cardini's stage characterization of an aloof, monocled, highly respectable English gentleman.

In 1916, a bomb exploded near Pitchford. At first he was believed dead. Miraculously, another soldier detected a breath of life, and Pitchford was sent to an army hospital. His convalescence was long and slow. To pass the time, Pitchford began to work with magic. When he requested a deck of cards, the nurses were understanding. But when he asked for a pair of white gloves, they sent him to the mental ward. The psychiatrists determined that he wasn't insane, and Pitchford made his

Much to Cardini's annoyance, troublesome lighted cigarettes multiplied of their own accord in his hands.

debut performing magic for the amusement of the other patients. By the time he was discharged 18 months later, Pitchford had decided to become a professional magician.

Pitchford was not immediately successful, and 1918 found him demonstrating tricks behind the magic counter of a department store in London. He decided to travel to Australia for his health (he was to remain weak throughout his life). In Sydney his act was a hit at the Tivoli, one of the largest theaters in that city. During this time, Cardini performed a talking routine featuring cards, scarves,

the same Chicago hotel. Some weeks later, she encountered him again on vacation in Michigan. Fascinated by the handsome performer, Swan went backstage and introduced herself. The two had a whirlwind four-week courtship and were married. They remained married for 47 years, until Cardini's death in 1973.

Shortly after the wedding Swan joined the act as Cardini's assistant. At first little changed. As she remembers, "I dressed up the act a little." But when other magicians also began featuring thimbles and scarves, Cardini dropped them in

Cardini's monocle became his trademark—even more than the white gloves he wore while accomplishing his manipulations.

and diamond-studded thimbles under the stage name, Val Raymond. An American competitor was billing himself as The Great Raymond; an Australian agent suggested that Pitchford select another alias. He became Cardini.

Cardini first came to the United States in 1926. He arrived on the West Coast and was still presenting his talking routine with thimbles and scarves. Things changed considerably when he met Swan Walker en route to New York. Swan had first seen Cardini while they were both working at

favor of billiard balls and cigarettes. He stopped talking during his routine and began pantomiming instead. They hit on the idea of dressing Swan in the costume of a page boy.

The new act began with Swan calling, "Paging Mr. Cardini! Paging Mr. Cardini!" Cardini entered absentmindedly reading a newspaper. He was impeccably dressed in top hat, tails, a purple-lined cape, and white gloves. He carried a cane and sported a monocle. He was extremely aloof and dignified. As Cardini handed his newspaper to the

page, he was startled and annoyed to discover card fans materializing in his hands. He threw one handful after another into the newspaper, but the cards continued to appear.

No sooner was Cardini freed from the cards than he was similarly plagued by billiard balls. Suddenly eight of them appeared between the fingers of his hands. Sometimes Cardini was so shocked by these strange proceedings that the monocle fell out of his eye. With a show of disgust, he shook crop after crop of billiard balls from his fingers.

At last the billiard balls subsided; Cardini decided to relax with a smoke. It proved exactly the wrong thing to do. Lighted cigarettes began to appear in mad profusion. He hardly had time to take a puff before more burst forth between every pair of fingers. He threw one batch down and stamped them out as another appeared. At last, when he had discouraged the cigarettes and was momentarily at ease, he found himself confronted by a smoking cigar. The cigar was followed by a meerschaum pipe. Cardini plucked the pipe out of the air and left the stage puffing on it.

In spite of the extraordinary nature of his props, Cardini maintained the cool composure of an unflappable gentleman. He remained withdrawn, seeming slightly bored by the proceedings and perhaps a shade intoxicated. Elegantly slim and tall, he had the appeal of a movie star. In his book, *Greater Magic*, John Northern Hilliard describes him as being "as graceful as Fred Astaire."

Richard and Swan Cardini entertained throughout the United States and Europe. In London they appeared for ten consecutive months at the Palladium and gave a command performance for English royalty. In New York the couple was booked for repeat performances at Radio City Music Hall and the Palace Theater. Cardini had the distinction of being one of the few magicians to headline a variety bill at the Palace.

In the early years, the Cardinis traveled around the country in a trailer which they preferred to hotel life. Eventually, they bought a house in Jamaica, New York. There they raised two children, a boy and a girl. In 1966, the couple retired to a summer home in northern New York State. Cardini died there in 1973.

In the film **Judex**, Channing Pollock plays a dashing avenger of evil. Early in the drama he performs magic, while disguised, at a masquerade ball. In this strange setting his moody dove productions become darkly symbolic.

CHANNING POLLOCK

Handsome as a Hollywood star, Pollock aspired to become an actor. He made several films in which he did not perform magic.

Dove manipulations were introduced to the United States in the 1940's by Cantu, a Mexican magician who produced a dove at the conclusion of each of his effects. But a few years later, such manipulations became identified with a handsome young magician named Channing Pollock, who had developed a unique style of his own. His dove act became one of the most widely imitated magic acts in the world—but few of the imitators could duplicate his artistry.

In fact, Pollock was impossible to imitate because the excitement of his routine was inherent in his personality. He is a strikingly handsome man, projecting the dark romanticism of a screen star. When he performed on stage, he made the most of his handsome features. He never smiled through the course of a performance; only at the conclusion did he deign to offer the audience a fleeting grin.

On their own, birds are lovely; used as magic props they are particularly arresting. Their fluttering wings create a dramatic contrast with the inanimate objects surrounding them. A scarf which lies immobile on a magician's hand suddenly bursts into life and movement. When Pollock used doves, they became more than pretty bird productions. The entire act had a richly symbolic character.

Both Pollock and his assistant were dressed in black. Their clothing was meant to contrast with the white doves and bright red silks which were the routine's major props. When Pollock made a dove materialize, he seemed to be sculpting it with his hands. He worked slowly and his large hands seemed invested with a miraculous strength. His ability as an actor enabled him to create a mood of real magic.

This ability to create art and emotion and establish an aura of mystery is one mark of the greatest conjurers. Pollock left a lasting impression on magic. Even after his retirement in 1969, his stature remains virtually undiminished.

On stage Pollock was famous for never smiling while he manipulated cards and doves.

When Richard Ross performs the mystery of the Chinese Linking Rings, solid steel becomes penetrable. He moves very slowly as he works. The ring in his left hand apparently passes unobstructed to link onto the ring in his right.

RICHARD ROSS

1. Not only are the magic rings able to link and unlink at Ross's discretion, they also apparently dissolve momentarily.

2. The only possible way for him to draw an entire ring through another is for one of them to dematerialize.

Richard Ross walks onto the stage in a well-tailored navy blue tuxedo. A small white-and-gold pedestal holding an ornate white jewel box awaits him. Tall, young, blond and blue-eyed, he bows and smiles at the audience. He is cool and elegant, words that describe both his polished good looks and his performance. Music begins as Ross takes a stack of rectangular white papers from his pocket. Turning himself and the papers, he shows the audience that they are white on both sides. He folds the stack in half and in his hands the papers turn green, then become a stack of bills. He folds the bills in half. About to put them away, he is surprised to discover a large gold coin tucked inside. He opens his jewel box, drops the bills inside, and holds the glittering coin in two fingers so his viewers can examine it.

Thus begins Ross's version of a classic trick, the Miser's Dream. It is an effect that has been performed on the stage and in the streets for hundreds of years, but Ross makes it as lyrical as a dance. He moves slowly. The coins appear, not in gleaming profusion, but in a majestic procession. He reaches into the air and extracts one gold coin, then another and another. He drops them from his long, graceful fingers into the box. Still more hang in the air, waiting for him to find them. Then he reaches, finds nothing, offers the audience a look of confusion, and turns to pull a coin from its invisible location behind him. He smiles to let the audience know it was there all along.

As the music changes to a concerto, Ross allows the remaining coins to stay hidden, presumably to be harvested later. He opens a small drawer in his table and extracts a shining ring, holding it in both hands as he exhibits it to the audience. He finds another, then two more. Unlike more traditional presentations of the Linking Rings effect, Ross uses only four. He handles them in the same slow and delicate manner that he used to gather the coins. The rings never clank roughly together;

rather they fall upon each other with the sound of wind chimes. Slowly, he raises one ring and draws another the identical size through it. It is physically impossible to pass one circle through another at right angles—one ring must distort. Yet they pass noiselessly, unchanged. The metal appears to have briefly dissolved, then resolidified. The audience catches its breath. Linking three rings in a chain, Ross draws the fourth up and through each of the others. Mysteriously, it slides through one, then another, and finally the last, to end linked at the top. Ross smiles as the entranced audience applauds.

The gleaming rings appear to gain a life of their own. As Nate Leipzig's cards seemed more than cards when he made them dance and flow, so

1. Richard Ross's watches exhibit properties quite as unusual as the Linking Rings. They multiply effortlessly in his hands.

the rings seem almost to change their composition in Ross's hands. The audience is all the more mystified by the slow progression of his performance. It seems they have plenty of time to discover his secret, yet the rings continue to mystify as they magically link and unlink.

Finished with the rings, Ross soundlessly re-

places them in the drawer, closing it with his long fingers. He looks inside the box to see what else he will find. The music changes to a clock rhythm as he withdraws a large pocket watch. In his hands it becomes two, then three, finally four watches. He puts the extras away, but the remaining watch again multiplies. Suddenly, they begin sprouting grow golden chains. He places one handful, then another into the box, and with the last beat of the music extends one finger to close it with a small thump. He bows gracefully to acknowledge the audience's tumultuous applause.

Richard Ross is one of the best contemporary cabaret and stage magicians. His movements and choreography show the precision of many hours of practice, cool calculation, and enormous skill. The act is thoughtfully executed. One effect leads into another, and each movement flows into the next

2. From one watch comes two, three, four, five, and six. They are seemingly able to divide themselves endlessly. Each time Ross tries to divest himself of one handful, he finds he has another.

3. Suddenly the enlarged watches begin to develop golden chains. Watch after watch drops to dangle from Ross's fingers.

long golden chains. Soon pocket watches on chains, swinging in time to the tick-tock beat of the music dangle from Ross's every finger. As he tries to put the last watch away, it triples in size. He looks at it, smiles broadly at the audience and it becomes two, then three, and then he has a collection of enormous watches in his hands. They, too, begin to

clearly and logically. There is a mood of wonder and enchantment throughout Ross's performance which lingers long after he has left the stage.

In many ways, Ross gives a classical performance. He is elegantly dressed in formal attire, and his effects are based on traditional presentations. Yet, Ross is modern. His music is popular.

The stage is simple. He uses no magician's paraphernalia, no top hat or wand. His regal manipulations do not recall past performances as much as they create new impressions. The Linking Rings effect, one of the oldest in magic, gains new dimensions in Ross's hands. His interpretation is unique, because he uses only four rings instead of the more standard eight or ten. His coin production and watch multiplications are invested with contemporary simplicity. There are no gaudy elaborate displays in Ross's magic.

The visual impact Ross creates is strengthened by the austerity of his setting. He uses only a small table and a little box. He never strays from its side. He reaches only to remove or replace

Ross uses sound with equal skill. In addition to color, music accentuates and punctuates each effect. The musical accompaniment changes as he introduces each new prop. Also, the tempo of the music helps Ross key his movements. "Music is very important," he says. "If I get started wrong, I can unbalance the whole composition."

One quality that marks an artist, particularly a fine magician, is that he makes what he is doing look easy. As Ross works there is no suggestion of strain. His technique is so precise he is considered by many to be a magician's magician. His graceful movements demonstrate the

1. All that is necessary is for Ross to tap two rings lightly and they link together.

2. Ross links an additional ring to the first. As he spins the two hanging rings, the metal purrs from the contact.

something. In this way, he rivets attention on a very small portion of the stage, and, more importantly, on himself. His choice and use of color aid in creating dramatic intensity. Gold, silver, white, and blue combine to create a subtle but intense background of color. When small bits of green appear as white papers change into dollar bills, the sudden addition of a new color is startling.

reality of Robert Houdin's statement that a magician's "fingers have more need to move with deftness than with speed." The coins seem to be waiting to be found, watches multiply at the lightest touch of his fingers. Yet, Ross's cool manner never becomes cold. His affectation of surprise involves his audience. They, too, seem to enjoy the pleasure Ross takes in his work.

Ross began practicing magic as a sixteen-year-old in Holland. From a leisure activity it quickly blossomed into a full-time passion. "My parents weren't interested at first," he says. "Then they began to notice that my magic was more than a hobby for me. I bought one trick, then another. Soon I was spending all of my allowance on magic tricks. I forgot about school entirely. I didn't care about anything except magic."

As a youth, Ross was fascinated by the spellbinders, particularly by the magic of the famous Dutch conjurer Fred Kaps. Ross had chosen one of the finest magicians in the world to idolize, but he did not mimic his prestigious countryman. Kaps is tall and dark and performs his intricate manipulations with an elegant sense of humor. Ross's stage presence, concepts, and effects are original. As an amateur, Ross won top honors at the European F. I. S. M. (Fédération International des Sociétés Magiques) congress three times. With his final victory in 1974, he believed himself qualified to become a professional. The other magicians had been a stimulating and challenging audience for Ross, but working in television and in cabarets has slightly altered his opinion. "At first, I preferred to perform for magicians," he says. "I liked to be able to fool them. But the more I performed, the more I focused on the audience instead of the tricks. Now I prefer a lay audience; I appreciate their reactions. I enjoy entertaining them."

3. Ross grasps one of the two linked rings and allows the two other rings to fall into a chain.

4. Holding the chain in his left hand, he draws a fourth ring up through the other three to end with it linked at the top.

1. Flip Hallema's bald head seems to accentuate his black-and-white color scheme. His appearance on the stage is drawn from the traditions of mime, but the behavior of his props is strictly magical.

FLIP

Flip Hallema's special magic is composed of equal parts of pantomime and prestidigitation. He relies on mime techniques to develop a stage character during his routine. Hallema's act is accompanied specially composed piano music, which, together with his simple props and unaffected personality, turns the performance into more than a magic show. There are no cards, coins, or multicolored silks; nothing but a white wand evokes the magician. The style of the performance indicates Hallema's personal orientation to his art. "Magic is

in the things," he says. "When Harry Blackstone performed the Dancing Handkerchief effect, the magic was in the handkerchief. But to create such magic in things, the whole routine must appear magical. The magic then is in the whole performance, not just in the tricks. I think, for instance, that puppeteers can sometimes be more magical than magicians."

Dressed in black and white, Flip strolls on stage, seemingly unaware of his audience, nonchalantly playing a harmonica and minding his own business. His white cap is cocked jauntily over one eye. He puts away the harmonica and is suddenly surprised when he discovers a white wand in his hand. Almost immediately the wand becomes two. He considers this phenomenon with astonishment.

2. Happy-go-lucky Flip has constant trouble with his belongings. Much to his surprise, his hat suddenly divides into two.

3. No matter what Flip does, some odd things seem to happen. He merely touches his tie and it breaks in half.

4. "What's going on here?" Flip appears to be asking. The next thing he knows, his tie too has doubled.

Next, he pulls a red polka-dot handkerchief out of his pocket, and it doubles as well. Perplexed, he removes his cap to scratch his head. While he thinks over what has been happening, he discovers two caps in his hand.

The wand continues to tease Flip throughout the performance. It disappears just when he wants it, only to surprise him by mischievously appearing in his back pocket, poking him to attract his attention. An unmanageable red ring, appearing out of nowhere, stubbornly floats just above the wand when he tries to slip it over the end. At each new turn of events, Flip seems as surprised as his audience. He tears a tissue in pieces and then finds it restored. From this one tissue comes a profusion of others. Flip becomes quite carried away with

them, kicking a great pile into the air and watching them float over the stage. Eventually, the little character gathers up his belongings, tucks them neatly into a small black bag, pulls out his harmonica and wanders away.

Hallema's routine is not a standard magic act. Viewers do not sense the rearrangement of natural forces that usually indicates they are under the control of the conjurer. Instead, Hallema is himself manipulated by the magical powers within his possessions—the normal flow of the control is reversed. In disclosing that magic resides in his props, Flip creates an unusual performance.

Ultimately, the magic of any performance lies in the emotional response of the audience. Magic combines elements of both deception and entertainment. Successful magic is not created by the manipulator who foresakes entertainment for an exhibition of his dexterity or the personality who entertains but does clumsy tricks. But Flip

sions and creates a sense of enchantment about their powers. He never becomes irritated with their rebelliousness no matter how much they tease him. "Children love my act and I enjoy per-

defines a magical relationship between his props and himself that amuses as it deceives.

The enjoyment of Flip's character requires a certain lightness of heart, an ability to become part of the entertainment instead of waiting to be amazed. "I tried to create a character with which the audience can identify," he says. "I stood in front of the mirror and looked at myself and I knew it would have to be a comic character." His humor has a familiar everyman flavor. He is a person enmeshed in a private world where suddenly crazy things begin to happen. He is a bit reminiscent of Chaplin's little tramp who was constantly victimized by events beyond his control.

In his confusion, Flip is gentle, even endearing. He seems delighted by his belligerent posses-

forming for them," says Hallema. "If children like something, adults will like it too. But the reverse is not necessarily the case. I learn a great deal from children. I like to work at colleges and universities as well."

Hallema first became interested in magic in Holland at the age of nine. He continued conjuring as a hobby while he established himself in graphics and industrial design. While working full time as a designer, Hallema performed magic as often as possible. Eventually, magic and designing exchanged positions. Hallema began working full time as a magician with a designing job attracting him only occasionally.

Hallema's familiarity with graphics may account in part for the visual strength of his act. His costume and props are all black, white, and red. The colors are deceptively simple. The effect is uncluttered clarity. Hallema's appreciation of oriental philosophy also enriches his character's uncompli-

falls into its owner's hand when he says the word yes. While he stares at it in perplexity, Hallema holds out his hand. "Here," he says. "You keep the hole. Just be careful you don't fall into it."

Flip is confused and perplexed by the strange behavior of his wand. He cannot seem to subdue any of his possessions. The magic they evidence is as mysterious to Flip as it is to his audience.

cated reactions. "God," he says, "is in the details."

Hallema's love of his craft not only pervades his stage performances; it is equally apparent in the bits of impromptu magic he enjoys doing offstage. He carries some red rope in his pocket. Given the opportunity, he happily performs a play. He knots the rope in various shapes, perhaps settling on a pair of eyeglasses. He borrows a ring from one of the people watching him. "I have," he says, "a portable hole. I can put it wherever I want." He knots the ring securely on the rope. "Can you get it off?" he inquires. The owner of the ring makes an unsuccessful attempt to remove it. "No?" Well, if I just put the hole in the rope, the ring will come off." He inserts the invisible hole. "Now say yes, and the ring will come off." The ring

Hallema lives in Holland with his wife and small daughters. Most of the time he works in his native country, often at a local cabaret in the company of a singer and a political satirist. He also presents many shows for children. He is happy to work full time in magic. "I don't know how long I will have this good fortune," he says. "Perhaps some day I will have to go back to industrial designing. Or maybe I will tire of performing. Right now it seems incredible to me that I have toured the world lecturing and performing magic. I realized a childhood dream when I visited Japan and toured the United States. You can't appreciate another country unless you are able to go there. People all over the world have been wonderful to me."

Dick Zimmerman designed and constructed the props for his Magic Circles routine. He links and unlinks the giant rings at left in a unique variation of the ancient Linking Rings Effect. Here he watches as a little ring floats lightly above a piece of rope.

DICK AND DIANA ZIMMERMAN

Dick and Diana Zimmerman are the archetypical magician couple. Diana bought her first magic trick in Phoenix when she was eight. Encouraged by her father, she was presenting her own magic act by the time she was a teenager. Dick became interested in magic when he saw Harry Blackstone in Charleston, West Virginia. "I got a magic set when I was a kid," he says, "and I never lost any of the pieces." The couple met at an industrial trade show where they were both doing magic, and they were married under an arch of wands at the Magic Castle in Hollywood, California. "At the end of the ceremony Dick made me vanish in a puff of smoke," says Diana.

Dick Zimmerman is a versatile and talented man. He has an undergraduate degree in civil engi-neering and a master's degree in structural engineering from Stanford University. "After I got my graduate degree," he says, "I decided engineering was a nice major, but not something to do. I spent the next 12 years designing games and toys." Dick's interest in ragtime piano also competes with his magic. He recently recorded Scott Joplin's piano works, and he founded the Maple Leaf Club, an organization devoted to classic ragtime music. "But magic was always in the background as a semiprofession," he says. "More and more, it is becoming a full-time profession."

Diana Zimmerman has always been a full-time magician. She started doing magic in burlesque houses and later developed a cabaret act. In the late 1960s, she first performed her phonograph record act, in which she produces a succession of

Diana Zimmerman is one of the few professional woman magicians in the United States. Her unusual act is based on a phonograph record motif. She levitates a 45-rpm disk over a cloth.

brightly colored records which diminish until they become the size of quarters. She floats a full-sized record above a silk square and makes her pet Yorkshire terrier and a phonograph appear. "It's hard for a woman to succeed as a magician," she says. "Women must be better than men. I think more women could be magicians, but most don't want to devote the necessary time to it. Standing in front of a mirror for hours is hard work."

Diana acts as Dick's assistant when he performs his Magic Circles act, first presented at Milt Larsen's "It's Magic" show in Los Angeles in 1964. The act is composed primarily of small effects—a floating ring, the production of a series of small linked rings, and an enlarged version of the Linking Rings effect. Everywhere there are circles, even a supposedly full container of milk tumbles into circular segments. In the final effect, a large-scale illusion, Diana is made to appear inside a net of the large rings. It is an excellent act, and Dick's enthusiasm for his magic comes across on stage. "You can't be successful unless you can fool people," he says. "Of course, if you bore them to tears while you're fooling them, people won't care.

Good magic makes people care about it."

Although they both have separate routines, which each performs on stage, as well as on television, most of Dick and Diana's work comes from the industrial trade shows that have been a boon to performing magicians. For these events they work as a team to develop magic effects around products. "You can do magic with anything," says Diana. "A can of tuna fish, anything." Dick agrees. "Magic is a huge field," he says. "There are so many things you can do, especially in the industrial field. You are limited only by your own imagination."

Dick and Diana work out Diana's trade-show routines together. Dick then designs and builds the effects and Diana performs them. Their talents blend well. "The idea is to be able to apply principles of magic, whatever the situation is. An artist using the tools of his trade doesn't have to keep painting the same picture," says Dick. Diana brings an enthusiasm to her performances that evokes the spirit of the eight-year-old in Phoenix. She doesn't mind the rigors of travel and performances, she says, as long as Dick is with her.

MR. ELECTRIC

s Mr. Electric, Marvyn Roy epitomizes the modern magician's specialty act. He creates an original performance by means of unusual props: light bulbs. There are few absolutely new ideas in the mysterious arts, and even electricity was used in stage magic more than a century ago. But in Roy's hands, electricity becomes futuristic. His performance evokes the fantastic world of science fiction. Marvyn Roy—Mr. Electric—the man who can make light bulbs light with his bare hands.

Many of Roy's effects are magic classics that he has reworked to accommodate his electrical theme. Under new guises, old tricks are newly exciting, especially as performed by Mr. Electric. "No one," says Clarke Crandall in *Genii* magazine, "but Con Edison dares copy him." The routine begins with the production of a chandelier of lighted bulbs, a feat spectacular enough to be featured as the finale of many a cabaret act. Then Mr. Electric flourishes handfuls of small, round bulbs as colorful as Christmas lights. The bulbs change color and multiply in the manner of billiard balls. Mr. Electric also does a light-bulb version of the Egg Bag

Trick, the Milk Trick and the Needle Trick. Instead of an egg, he displays a light bulb in pristine condition after he supposedly smashed it to bits. In the Milk Trick, milk mysteriously vanishes only to reappear inside a clear large bulb instead of a more conventional container.

More astonishing is Mr. Electric's version of the Needle Trick. Instead of swallowing the traditional needles and thread, Roy gulps light bulbs and a length of electric cord. One by one, the bulbs reappear lit and strung in a seemingly endless, glowing procession. Seven pop out of his mouth, followed by a dozen more. Then he produces 19 more—an amazing 38 in all. Roy's wife and assistant, Carol, jumps backward with a drum beat as each bulb emerges and extends the string of lights across the darkened stage.

Mr. Electric's forte, however, is in turning on lights in impossible situations. He manages to light bulbs in water and in his bare hands. With spectacular dramatics, he takes a great bulb in one hand and lifts his other hand high in the air. As the theater darkens, he commands the energy of the cosmos. When he lowers his raised hand to grasp the bulb, the filament at first glows dimly. Slowly it

1. Mr. Electric (Marvyn Roy) prepares to light a 5000-watt bulb intended for use in a lighthouse.

2. As the theater darkens, Mr. Electric summons the energy of the atmosphere into his body.

3. Protected by special glasses, Mr. Electric causes the bulb to glow dimly and then brighten. In the darkness the illusion creates an eerie, other-worldly sensation.

brightens, increasing in brilliance as the tension in the hushed theater mounts. The current appears to emanate from Mr. Electric's body. Mr. Electric is able to light a 1000-watt bulb, then a 5000-watt bulb intended for use in a lighthouse.

If Roy is performing in small quarters or in the round, the 5000-watt bulb is his concluding effect. But if he is on a spacious stage, he caps his routine with a large-scale illusion. He makes Carol appear inside a giant light bulb with an enormous matching shade.

Roy is a tall, handsome man with wavy black hair and an expansive smile. He is buoyant and exuberant both on and off the stage. His routine is wordless and fast paced—Roy crackles with energy. Once described by another magician as being

1. Naturally, when Mr. Electric performs a multiplication, he uses lightbulbs instead of ordinary billiard balls.

Carol Roy pulls bulb after bulb from her husband's mouth. Eventually, the string spans the entire stage. How Roy manages to conceal more than three dozen light bulbs is a mystery.

"like a kid with a new magic set," he fires his audience with his own enthusiasm. Spectators cannot avoid becoming involved and he is delighted by their response. "You should see the people in front when I light the 5000-watt bulb," he says. "They pull back and sometimes even put up their arms to shield themselves."

Roy's energy and enthusiasm seem incredible, considering that he has performed his act for

2. One after another the colorful bulbs appear between Mr. Electric's fingers. The mystery is deepened by the fact that the bulbs are already glowing when they appear.

nearly 30 years. It has undergone many revisions and additions, but his approach remains remarkable. Roy sustains his enthusiasm because he is a natural extrovert, a born performer with a tailor-made routine. "In magic everything is in perspective," he says. "You have some who are great working in a cabaret, some who are great doing close-up magic, some who are great doing big illusions, and you also have amateurs who are better than many professionals. But there is a great gulf between an amateur and a professional. There is nothing wrong with being an amateur, but a professional has to be commercial all the time. An amateur can please only himself, but we can't. So you'll find that a pro, a full-time pro who has been working for 20 years, develops an approach that

hood. In 1939 he won acclaim at a San Francisco magic convention as a teenager, and by the 1940s was a professional magician. While a soldier in World War II he first had the notion of presenting an act with light bulbs. Later in the decade, he developed his light-bulb routine, and by the early 1950s the act was successful.

Roy met Carol Williams while on tour with a variety show on ice. He was playing in Chicago when agent Muriel Abbott asked him to do the act on skates. Roy didn't know how to skate at the time, but he decided to learn. It was an advantageous decision. In Phoenix, Arizona, he met Carol, who was a professional ice skater. They married and have been performing together ever since.

For many years Marvyn and Carol Roy per-

1. Holding an armful of scarves aloft, Mr. Electric begins a spectacular trick in which an object will materialize.

2. Who else but Mr. Electric could produce a brilliantly glowing, fully lighted electric chandelier?

fits him best and makes his product unique. People may say that it's only a gimmick, or it's a specialty act, and that people forget my name. But they remember Mr. Electric. In the old days, when many magicians were competing for work, an agent would snap his fingers and say, 'Get me the guy with the light bulbs.' No one else was doing an act with electricity. We developed it over the years. So now if you want Mr. Electric you have to get Mr. Electric. You can't do what others have done and hope to succeed. You have to create. Of course, there are classic illusions, but you have to develop your own version. The vital thing in magic is the secret, the magic. If a magician is good, everybody says, 'How did he do that?'"

Roy has been involved in magic since child-

formed almost exclusively in Europe, where they found receptive audiences. Then they bought a home in southern California and decided to travel less. Their extensive globe-trotting has sometimes accounted for amusing confusion about the Roys. During their first European engagement at the Lido in Paris in 1954, they received an invitation to appear on Ed Sullivan's television program. Sullivan wanted to book the fabulous "French" magician with the light bulbs. When the Roys returned to the United States in the early 1970s to tour North America, the press was similarly mistaken. Roy chuckles as he recalls the reviews: "After we came back to America, people said, 'Here's a fantastic new magician.' After 30 years, I found myself described as a new magician."

NORM NIELSEN

Magicians have based their performances on many themes. Both T. Nelson Downs and Channing Pollock developed acts founded on props; Cardini used character and Norm Nielsen uses a musical motif. Nielsen relates his effects to one another in terms of an idea, rather than an object or a personality. His effects are standard—there is a levitation, a disappearance, a coin production, and a card production—but fresh and exciting. His act is a well-executed dramatic whole. Nielsen establishes himself on stage, builds to his main effect, the Floating Violin, then finishes with a spectacular version of the Miser's Dream. The entire performance shines with the professional polish that results only from hard work and experience.

Like so many magicians, Nielsen as a youngster of twelve or thirteen was inspired by a local conjurer in his home town in Wisconsin. "There was a town barber who did magic," he says. "This fellow used to go from one bar to the next doing magic, and I used to follow him around." Inevitably, Nielsen began to create his own mysteries. He practiced through adolescence and eventually de-

1. In keeping with his theme of musical magic, Norm Nielsen begins to play a melody on a magic flute.

2. Before he can blow a single note, Nielsen is seized by a violent urge to sneeze.

3. As he sneezes, Nielsen's flute disintegrates into hundreds of tiny silver fragments.

veloped a cabaret act. When he realized he could not make ends meet performing, he opened a magic shop in Kenosha, Wisconsin. Nielsen built and sold various tricks and illusions, perfecting the skills of magic construction that later enabled him to build his own effects.

The idea of Musical Magic developed from Nielsen's early routines over the course of several years. His first brainstorm was the Floating Violin. "I was doing an act with a floating ball and a cloth, an old Thurston effect," he says. "I thought, 'Why wouldn't this trick work with something more interesting than balls?' At first I thought of a trumpet, but I decided people wouldn't be able to see the keys moving. Then I built the violin—a couple of times." After he had completed a good work-

4. Nielsen takes a complacent attitude. "Oh well," he seems to say, "some days are better than others."

ing model of the violin, Nielsen created an entire set around it. Naturally, the evolution of the act as a whole also took place over a period of time.

Nielsen's Floating Violin is considered one of the finest effects presented in magic today. It is as gracefully performed as it is beautifully constructed. As the effect begins, the music accompanying Nielsen fades. The stage is left silent as he brings out the violin. At first, it seems that he is going to play it himself, but then both the violin and its bow float away in the air. The bow moves across the strings and sweet music issues from the instrument. As the violin drifts above Nielsen's magic cloth, it seems to acquire a personality of its own. From time to time the violin dips below the cloth as if it were somewhat shy of performing before an audience. "Come on, come on," Nielsen mouths, nodding his head in encouragement as one might cajole a reticent child. It returns, plays its music, and charms the audience.

Although the rest of Nielsen's routine is built around this effect, he begins the performance with a nonmusical card production. "I start off with the cards to establish myself as a magician," he says. "People like to see card tricks. When I first put the act together I used to start with a page of music and break it into pieces the size of playing cards. I would throw the musical cards into a music box that wouldn't play until they were inside. But the effect was too contrived, too excessive. I decided to use ordinary playing cards instead and worked out a special card production. People like it better." Nielsen's method of producing cards is unique. Instead of plucking them out of the air like other magicians, he makes cards appear in his folded hands. It is an interesting variation. With this method, Nielsen is able to face his audience while he produces the cards.

Nielsen finishes with his special version of the Miser's Dream. He pulls coins from thin air at an increasingly faster pace until coins seem to be pouring from his fingers. But as the coins appear, he drops them down a vertical xylophone. The first coins make tinkling scales as they fall and as more and more follow, a numismatic melody begins. Golden coins fall down the golden keyboard in a glittering finish to a jewellike routine.

1. Nielsen's central effect is his fabulous Floating Violin. The instrument rests on his arm while he places the bow upon it.

Norm Nielsen is a soft-spoken, quietly confident person, and his stage presence reflects his off-stage composure. He is professionally suave in the tradition of Cardini and Pollock but with a casual, contemporary manner. Nielsen never hurries on stage. Calm and smiling, he evidences a reserved but friendly attitude. Nielsen dresses formally but in current styles. The sparkle of a stick pin sets off his ruffled shirt and his curling, longish blond hair completes a picture of modern elegance. He appears handsome and debonair—and approachable.

Nielsen performs almost exclusively in Europe. He finds the European cabaret circuit offers him consistently better rewards than its counterpart in the United States. Nielsen was offered work in France while he was performing

3. The little violin exhibits its own personality as it dips and glides above Nielsen's magic cloth.

with Mitzi Gaynor in Las Vegas—while in Nevada he was booked for a nine-month run in Paris. "It is possible," he says, "to work seven days a week in Europe. Each major city has at least one big nightclub, and most have several. The engagements generally run about one month each, long enough so the traveling is not much of a strain. In general, I think Europeans take magic more seriously than Americans. In the United States there is more interest in amateurs and semiprofessionals, but there are few places to present a cabaret act. Las Vegas, Reno, and Miami are about the only places left." Though Nielsen seldom returns to his home country, his reputation increases in his absence. Other magicians speak of him in the deferential tones his beautiful act deserves.

2. At Nielsen's command, both bow and violin float in the air. The instrument miraculously begins to play a melodious tune.

Nielsen concludes with a musical version of the Miser's Dream. As he turns his head from left to right, he materializes coins behind his ears and drops them down a vertical xylophone. He works faster and faster as he builds to a glittering, tinkling finish.

THE GREAT TOMSONI

Johnny Thompson had been to a lot of places and seen a lot of things before he created the Great Tomsoni—the celebrated Polish magician who is beset by minor accidents on the Las Vegas stage. He first became fascinated by the art of illusion in Chicago at the age of eight. "I saw a motion picture, *Mississippi River Boat* with Tyrone Power," he recalls. "I rushed to buy *The Expert at the Card Table*. I spent the next four years mastering everything in the book, then had a rude awakening when I discovered that there aren't many places for a twelve-year-old card cheat to go. So I started doing magic tricks. I got a job at Riverside Amusement Park in Chicago in a ten-in-one show—a freak show. I told them I was fourteen. They were doing 12 to 18 shows a day. I lasted only two weeks. There was a dwarf in the company called Waldo the Human Ostrich. Waldo swallowed things, then regurgitated them intact. He would swallow a goldfish and a white rat, then a whole lemon. In the middle of the second week Waldo got the lemon wedged in sideways, turned blue and keeled over. I called an ambulance. They pumped his stomach and that killed his rat and his fish. Waldo was furious. I didn't know I was only supposed to pound him on the back if the lemon got stuck.

"After that I got a job with the Great Garrison as a magician's assistant. That was in the early 1950s. I worked at county fairs, spent another summer in a ten-in-one show, then finally graduated to grandstand shows. I was doing quite well in small towns of the Midwest. Then I saw Cantu, the Mexican dove manipulator. I thought his act was beautiful, and I developed a bird act of my own. But Channing Pollock appeared on Ed Sullivan's television show with his dove act. There wasn't room for two such routines."

Temporarily out of ideas, Thompson returned to one of his other professions—harmonica player. He was one of the original Harmonicats. After leaving them in 1957, he founded his Harmonica

Jazz Quartet. Unfortunately, the audience for jazz harmonica wasn't large. "Harmonica players," says Thompson, "were turned off by the jazz and jazz musicians were turned off by the harmonicas."

By the early 1960s, Thompson was again performing magic. "There were thousands of bird acts in imitation of Channing Pollock," he says. "Agents would say, 'What do you do?' I'd say, 'I produce birds.' They didn't even want to look at the act."

(Above) The knot the Great Tomsoni has tied in the scarf mysteriously drops out. There is nothing up his sleeve to assist him, at least not in his coat sleeves.

1. (Right) Tomsoni, too seems surprised that he has produced a dove without mishap...yet.

Next, Thompson began building large illusions for trade shows and store windows. "I'm no businessman," he says. "I was losing money. I was doing magic shows so I could keep building those things. I soon discovered that I didn't want to be a jazz musician on the harmonica, nor did I want to be a purveyor of illusions for trade shows."

During this period, Thompson composed music for two comedians. Under their influence, he began to consider introducing comedy into his dove act. "I wanted to do comedy," he says, "but I also wanted to do strong magic; so I had to come up with a premise. The people who were copying Pollock usually were not as handsome as he. He never smiled until the end of his act. Other people would

2. The Great Tomsoni must be the most accident-prone magician in the business.

3. No matter how hard he tries to maintain his dignity, fate seems pitted against him.

try to do the same, but they had to make up for the difference in comeliness by adopting an arrogant attitude. I decided to use this affected arrogance to create a humorous character. The Great Tomsoni constantly has accidents on stage. But whenever anything goes wrong, he overcomes it by sheer arrogance, acting as if nothing has happened. I do three things to establish the Channing Pollock image, and the rest of the act is my own. All the accidents that happen to Tomsoni have happened to me at one time or another."

Almost from the very moment the Great Tomsoni walks on stage, his act runs amok. He enters wearing a tuxedo and top hat and carrying a cane. The cane turns into a little stand, on which he places his hat in proper magician's fashion. He makes a scarf appear and produces a dove. His assistant arrives on stage but instead of taking both the dove and the scarf, she takes only the scarf. Unaware that she has left the stage Tomsoni hands her the dove. Noticing at last that she has departed, he puts the dove on the rim of his hat. By this time the audience has begun to titter. Tomsoni is aware of their mirth and his manner becomes increasingly haughty. His assistant returns to whisper that his fly is open. He steadfastly refuses to be embarrassed but looks progressively more sour. He knots a scarf, then lets the trick knot drop out to the sound of a drum roll. The drummer goes on and on. Tomsoni tries to maintain his composure at first, then gives the drummer a murderous look. With an ingratiating smile, he shows the audience that he is not the least bit concerned.

Tomsoni now becomes completely preoccupied with the dove still perched on his hat. His assistant brings him a handful of scarves. As he takes them from her one by one, he is paying so little attention to what he is doing that he somehow manages to catch hold of her dress. It comes off in his hand and she flees the stage. When Tomsoni reaches for a scarf that isn't there, he discovers his assistant's absence—and her dress in his hand. Thinking he has made her vanish, he smiles and bows deeply to the audience.

Now things turn from terrible to impossible. Tomsoni's assistant is furious. She contemptuously stomps on and off the stage in a bathrobe. Belligerently chewing gum, she refuses to look at him. As he suavely reaches for a scarf with two extended fingers, she throws it at him. He has to pick it up from the floor. The last scrap of dignity vanishes as Tomsoni announces his grand effect—the Babushkas of Warsaw—in a high-pitched, unsteady voice. Nonetheless, he carries on to the end, never relinquishing his increasingly ridiculous posture.

Although Thompson's routine is modern vaudeville, almost slapstick comedy, it allows him to realize his goal of performing strong magic. The Great Tomsoni is a carefully constructed character. Though the relentless hand of fate turns his every action into absurdity, his magic effects do not fail. Tomsoni is not a bungler; he suffers from an inflated ego. He cannot for a moment maintain the darkly symbolic mood of Channing Pollock's dove act, but he is quite unaware of this fact. He takes himself very seriously. The comedy in this arrogant posturing is underlined by the success of Tomsoni's magic. Without good magic, he would become a buffoon. With good magic, he is shortsighted, pretentious, overbearing, and hilarious. Humor has given Thompson's fine work the necessary dash and appeal to make it both original and commercial. The act has been successful for him.

"I am happy with what I do," says Thompson. "I think if you can create something original and devote enough time to perfecting it, there will always be work. I know I have 27 laughs in my act. I know they will all be there and I know why the laughs work. I also know why the magic works, and that's what takes the most time to learn."

1. The Great Tomsoni concludes his act with the unexpected appearance of a bowling ball.

2. As he bowls the ball into the wings, an enormous crash of bowling pins is heard. It sounds like a strike.

CARL BALLANTINE

Carl Ballantine walks on stage with a loose-kneed, bent-elbowed gait, his piercing blue eyes darting at the audience. He slams his table down and carelessly hangs up his banner. "Ballantine, it proclaims, "THIS WORLD'S GREATEST magician." He straightens, pausing for a moment, and gazes serenely over the audience. "Every move a picture," he sighs, stroking his lapel.

"Now let's get organized," he shouts, grabbing a small yellow basket and digging into it, "or we'll be here all night." He removes a piece of rope from the basket. "The magician," he announces sonorously as he draws himself up, "cuts the rope in half. Two pieces," he reminds the audience. He cuts the rope. "Ta, ta!" he crows, shaking his head and smiling at himself. "Ah," he says fondly, "this kid's dynamite."

1. Ballantine dusts off an ancient trick—he attempts to pull a rabbit out of a tall top hat.

2. "I'm coming down, boy!" Ballantine cries excitedly before plunging his arm into the hat. But he doesn't find a rabbit.

Carl Ballantine specializes in tricks that do not work. Neither he nor his audience knows what he might find in his magician's basket. "What's this," he asks, "a chicken in a basket?" He hurls the fowl over his shoulder in disgust.

"It's a simple trick, sticking the two hunks of rope back together again," he intones. "Keep your eye on the two hunks of rope." He spins around and hunches storklike over his basket with his elbows and knees protruding. The audience, unable to see anything but Ballantine's back, breaks up. "It's the only way I know," he shouts over his shoulder in distress. "Don't get mad."

For all of Ballantine's frantic efforts, he cannot restore the severed rope. Furious, he storms about the stage and shouts into the wings. "I'll tell them what happened. I ain't afraid." He returns to the audience with righteous indignation. "Some crumb back there cut them both.

"Sure gets the act off to a bad start," he says confidentially. He leans on his table and is momentarily calm. "Maybe I'm not the greatest," he continues, lifting his eyebrows and looking down his nose, "but I *am* the best dressed."

Ballantine also attempts the Torn and Restored Newspaper trick but he is no handier with newspapers than with ropes. He is too impatient to tear it meticulously. "There's a faster way," he mutters darkly—and ends by littering the stage with shredded newsprint. Kicking it aside, he steps forward with one hand on his chest. "By request," he intones grandly, "the rabbit from the top hat—always something new." Unceremoniously, he dumps the basket on the floor and slams down a battered top hat to replace it. He stuffs his arm into the hat up to his shoulder, thus revealing the false bottom in his table. "What's the matter?" he shouts at the audience as it roars with laughter. "If you're going to watch that close, I don't need this job." The audience never sees a rabbit, of course, and soon the hat goes flying across the stage.

Ballantine pulls a deck of cards from his pocket. "I'll do a few card tricks for you that I recorded a couple of years ago for Decca Records," he says. He blows into the cards and a harmonica sounds. "Playing cards," he says. "What will they think of next?" He extends one arm and bends slightly at the knees as he spreads the cards along his sleeve. "My favorite sleeve job...the cards march up the sleeve, flop over and stop like Pike's Peak," he says. The cards do nothing of the sort. He throws them on the floor in disgust.

1. Ballantine's opening trick is the Cut and Restored Rope. Throughout the routine he returns to it as a running gag.

By the end of his routine, Ballantine stands in a clutter of destroyed props. Bits of paper, a tray, the cards, the basket, the top hat—plus a large broom thrown in from the wings—are strewn about. His sign is completely cockeyed. "In conclusion..." he begins, mimicking the silver tones of a lecturer. Rapidly shifting to his own style, he ends by saying, "The nice thing about this act, when it dies I'm dressed for it."

Carl Ballantine discovered magic as a child in Chicago. "A barber used to come to our house and entertain me with thimble tricks while he cut my hair," he says. "Later on, when he saw my act, he said, 'I can't believe I started that.'" A magic trick hasn't worked properly for Ballantine since 1940. At that time he billed himself as The River Gambler and performed straight magic, with poker chips, playing cards, and money. "The act wasn't success-

2. After cutting the rope, Ballantine places the two pieces in his basket and makes mysterious passes over it.

3. Ballantine finally enjoys a modicum of success. "Almost!" he says, finding the halves joined by a slender thread.

ful in nightclubs," he says. "I had to make a living, so I looked at myself in the mirror and said, 'You don't look much like a magician.' Then I put this other thing together." The "other thing" soon became one of the most successful of contemporary magic acts. Ballantine's humor is show stopping. The jokes come so fast the audience can hardly absorb them. He carries out his noisy, vaudeville-style performance perfectly.

The apparent chaos on stage conceals a precise attention to detail and Ballantine's thorough knowledge of magic. "I don't do comedy magic," he says. "I do satire. There is a difference." Satire is topical humor which lampoons the foibles of its subject. The greater one's knowledge of a topic, the funnier a satire becomes. It is not necessary to be an expert on magic to appreciate Ballantine's satire, but some knowledge increases its richness.

When Ballantine started his routine, it was sometimes confusing to his audience. "I struggled for about five years," he says. "I had a tough time selling the act. The audience didn't know what I was trying to do. People thought I was either a bad magician or a bad comedian. Magic wasn't very popular in those days, and that made it harder. I used to follow myself—I'd play the Paramount in New York in January and return in August, and no other magician had played in the meantime. I was doing a satire on magicians and the audience assumed this was the way all magicians worked. I used to say, 'Book a magician, make it easier for me.' Later it became much easier. Magic increased in popularity. When I came on, the audience knew what was happening."

Making tricks fail is harder than it seems. Ballantine's tricks must not work, but they must not work in a way that mocks a straight magic performance. Yet, the gags must be funny to laymen as well as magicians. When Ballantine lifts a trouser leg and pulls out a paper bag, few in the audience know he is mocking a standard magic act, but

1. Ballantine begins the Torn and Restored Newspaper effect traditionally enough.

2. But Ballantine is much too impatient to tear the paper neatly. ("If I tear it straight, I ruin the gag," he says.)

it is funny anyway. When he says he is going to materialize a pigeon inside the bag (all Ballantine ever gets is a feather) they continue to laugh. It is not necessary to know that he is skillfully poking fun at countless dove manipulators or that he is breaking the magician's cardinal rule of never telling an audience what he is about to do before he does it.

Ballantine's magic works in part because he is so knowledgeable in the field. He makes fun of stuffy traditions as only a true insider can.

His magic also works because he is naturally a comedian. His every move on stage is funny. And although he is satiric, Ballantine is never caustic, nor does he wish to be. "I couldn't do what I am doing unless I loved magic," he says. "I don't do it vitriolically, I do it with love."

When not performing his magic, Ballantine has had various acting jobs. Most notably, he spent four years as a member of the cast of ABC television's *McHale's Navy*.

3. Murmuring incantations, Ballantine stuffs the newspaper scraps under an old-fashioned magician's tray.

4. The tray hits the stage with a reverberating clang and newspaper bits go flying in the air when Ballantine discovers he is unable to restore the paper to one piece. "Are you kidding?" he shouts.

LARGE-SCALE ILLUSIONS

A large-scale illusion is nearly always a stage effect. In general, a large-scale illusion uses equipment that is too large for one man to carry about (it won't fit in a suitcase) and often requires more than one person to execute it. Such a large-scale illusion is presented with the aid of equipment designed and constructed to produce the effect of an impossible happening. Large-scale illusions as they are presented on stage today are a comparatively recent development—they belong to a mechanical age and require the inventive faculties of watchmakers and engineers. Of course, their roots, like the roots of all magic, can be traced to the dawn of history. When priest-magicians covered themselves with the skins of animals and wore horns on their heads, they were in effect transforming themselves in much the same way a magician might change a man into a lion on a modern stage. Indian fakirs who were buried alive and exhumed days later unharmed (after tunneling in and out of the grave), the leaping altar fires of the Egyptians, even the Trojan Horse are examples of ancient large-scale illusions. But they bear little resemblance to the effects seen on stage today. Modern large-scale illusions owe most of their development to the great interest that magicians of the late eighteenth and early nineteenth centuries developed in mechanical contrivances.

From the beginning of the fourteenth century, conjurers made use of machinery of some sort in their illusions. Magicians who presented more elaborate effects based on mechanical devices were called *tregetours* to differentiate them from the sleight-of-hand artists of the time. In those early days any apparatus used by a magician was very basic and not particularly sophisticated in construction. Chaucer describes fantastic illusions produced by a *tregetour* in *The Franklyn's Tale*. If the effects he describes actually took place, they could have only been produced by a magic lantern. But the magic lantern was not invented until the seventeenth century. Since lenses of reasonable quality were available in the fourteenth century, it is surmised that *tregetours* may have presented telescopic and microscopic effects.

During the fifteenth and sixteenth centuries, the need for sophisticated tools for navigation furthered the development of horology. Watchmakers began to build automata as demonstrations of their skill. By the seventeenth and eighteenth centuries, clockmakers all over Europe were constructing mechanical eagles, harpsichord players, rope dancers, and the like, as well as fully mechanized reproductions of such establishments as bakeries and inns. Probably the most famous builder of automata was Jacques de Vaucanson, who exhibited his mechanical marvels at the Royal Academy of Sciences in Paris in 1738. It was about this time that these devices found a role in magic.

It was easy to rationalize including an automaton in a magic act—a good automaton was a mystery in itself. By having a mechanical man answer questions put to it by spectators, it was possible to create the illusion of a thinking machine. As it happened, some of the mechanical marvels were not so marvelous. In many cases, the lifelike movements of the machine were caused by the live movements of a child within.

At a booth at London's Bartholomew Fair in the early eighteenth century, Isaac Fawkes exhibited automata built by Christopher Pinchbeck, a clockmaker. Some 50 years later, Pinetti traveled with automata called Grand Sultan and Wise Little Turk. One of the most famous automata of all time, however, was a chess-playing Turk built by a Hungarian Baron Wolfgang von Kempelen. In the late eighteenth century, von Kempelen's chess master was acclaimed throughout Europe for its brilliance. The principle was simple: an excellent chess player was concealed inside.

By the early nineteenth century, exhibitions of mechanical wizardry were so popular that real conjuring was in danger of being eclipsed. The notable exception was the French magician Philippe. As the curtain opened at the beginning of his show, the stage was in total darkness. At the sound of a pistol shot, dozens of candles burst simultaneously into flame. Philippe went on to perform excellent magic. Most conjurers of the time, however, belonged to what Sidney Clarke, in *The Annals of Conjuring*, called "the decorative school of magic" in an "age of the tinsmith and the cabinet maker." Their stages were crowded with fantastic-looking equipment, strange boxes and complicated apparatus, but little really happened. Any compliments belonged to the builders, not to the ingenuity or artistry of the conjurers.

Because he was a watchmaker before he became one of history's great magicians, Robert-Houdin had a passion for automata. In the mid-nineteenth century half of his evening's show was filled with the presentation of such devices. He built a nightingale that, in his opinion, sang as sweetly as a real bird. He also built an entire automated confectioner's shop. But Houdin launched a new era in the art of magic when he employed his mechanical skill to build innovative equipment for use in effecting large-scale illusions.

By the end of the nineteenth century illusion shows were beginning to dominate magic. John Nevil Maskelyne, probably the most inventive magician the world has ever seen, performed with David Devant, George Cooke, and Bautier de Kolta at the Egyptian Hall in London. Maskelyne's shows were so original that rivals tried to sabotage them. They got his assistants drunk and tried to steal his secrets. Maskelyne concentrated on and obtained hundreds of patents on his various machines.

Maskelyne constructed one of the most famous of the magical mechanical men, Psycho. He bought the device, which performed a few simple movements, and set up a large workshop (the first of many Maskelyne workshops) to improve the original mechanism. He worked for two years on the automaton, and his results were spectacular. Psycho could nod, give the Mason's grip, add, multiply, divide, perform his own small conjuring tricks, spell, smoke cigarettes, and play whist. He gained considerable notoriety for his whist playing—Psycho almost always won.

At about the same time, Alexander Herrmann left his native Germany to make his home in the United States. Herrmann was primarily known for his sleight-of-hand effects but he slowly began to add large-scale illusions to his show. He became the most famous magician in the United States. His principal rival, Harry Kellar, presented a show with a different emphasis. He performed no sleight of hand at all but concentrated entirely on illusions. While Herrmann toured the United States, Kellar toured the world.

By the time the era of the great touring road shows began, magicians had successfully surmounted the problems of stage presentation. In doing so, they had overcome the difficulties of satisfying a larger and more distant audience. Now the challenge was to be original, and success followed the man who could create larger illusions for greater effect. An illusion show required railroad cars filled with equipment and scenery, plus dozens of assistants and costumes. Builders, maintenance men, and stage crews were needed. Magic became big business with both high risk and the potential of high rewards.

The large-scale illusions featured in such shows, and on the stage today, fall into four basic categories: suspensions and levitations; appearances and vanishes; the divided woman; and transformations. The variations possible in each class of illusion are endless, subject only to the limits of the magician's imagination, his technical skill, and the talent of his staff.

A levitation, the floating of an object or a person in the air, has its earliest roots in the legendary performances of Indian fakirs. Brahmin priests recorded accounts of holy men who floated themselves in the air as early as the first century. Later, European travelers returned from the Far East with tales of similar phenomena.

In the early nineteenth century a troupe of Indian magicians performed in London. Soon news of a fakir able to lift himself several feet in the air while sitting cross-legged spread through magic circles. Intrigued, Robert-Houdin devised his Ethereal Suspension, which was considered even more spectacular than the fakir's. (In a suspension, some support remains beneath the floating object, but in a levitation, the person or object floats unsupported.) In Houdin's version, his son, Émile, stood on a box with poles beneath his arms. Houdin pantomimed putting the boy to sleep with ether. As the boy dozed, Houdin removed first the box, then one of the poles. Next, he lightly lifted Émile until he was parallel with the stage, supported only by a pole under his right elbow. Fumes of ether wafting through the theater intensified the effect. It was a smash hit.

In Berlin, Compars Herrmann presented his version of Robert-Houdin's illusion, calling it the Horizontal Suspension and similarly treating his assistant with chloroform. Herrmann's biographers claim he invented the trick; Milbourne Christopher maintains that one of Robert-Houdin's workmen was eventually prosecuted for selling his employer's blueprints.

Later in the century, John Nevil Maskelyne perfected the levitation illusion. Maskelyne floated his assistant a few feet above the stage. Later, he presented his Levitation Extraordinary, in which he levitated himself high above the heads of his audience.

After the first waves of astonishment subsided, levitations sustained excitement with costumes, scenery, and suspenseful theatrics. For example, Herrmann played the evil hypnotist, Svengali, to his wife Adelaide's Trilby. Kellar's Levitation of Princess Karnac became famous, particularly when performed by Howard Thurston. Thurston sometimes floated the princess out over the audience and held her in the air for ten minutes while the audience, afraid to make a sound, barely breathed.

Appearances and vanishes are as common to the illusion show as levitations. The Indian Basket Trick is an ancient vanishing illusion with a subsequent reappearance, and Babylonian priests were adept at making food offerings disappear. In *The Discoverie of Witchcraft*, Reginald Scot describes a performance by a king's conjurer named Brandon who made a live bird appear from a picture.

Since these illusions are more flexible than levitations, they exist in greater variety. Perhaps the finest vanishing act ever presented on stage was devised by Bautier de Kolta in 1875. In his Vanishing Lady illusion, he seated his assistant on a chair and draped a large silk over her. Grasping her by the head, in a split second he made both girl and silk vanish, leaving only an empty chair on the stage. De Kolta also developed a cocoon illusion in which a girl suddenly burst from a large paper egg. He also held a birdcage and canary high in the air, then suddenly both vanished completely. In his Captive's Flight, a girl in the costume of a canary disappeared from a large bird cage.

Divided Woman effects include all the illusions which involve the division of an assistant into two or more parts. The classic illusion is Sawing-a-Woman-in-Half, first performed by P. T. Selbit in the 1920s with the woman in a box. (He performed it first with a male assistant but found that less effective.) Later, Horace Goldin did the trick using a buzz saw with the woman in full view. Maskelyne devised a comic rendition of a decapitation. Dressed as a barber, he inadvertently beheaded his customer, talked the situation over with his client's head, then restored him.

Less grisly is the modern divided woman, the ZigZag Girl, created in the 1960s by the English magician-inventor, Robert Harbin. It is a modern classic, ranking with Maskelyne's inventions in superior engineering and design. Like Maskelyne, Harbin is also acclaimed as a highly talented magician. In this case the woman is first trisected, then her midsection is moved to one side. In another variation, the Mismade Girl, a girl in a box is separated into quarters; then the segments are scrambled and arranged in a different sequence. Reopened, the boxes display the girl out of order.

Transformations, the final category of large-scale illusions, have been a favorite among magicians since Aaron changed the rod of Moses to a snake. In most modern versions, a person is changed into an animal and vice versa. Pumas, cheetahs, lions, and tigers are particularly exciting. One minute a smiling woman is in a cage, the next she is replaced by an awesome wild beast.

The classic transformation is the Metamorphosis. It was first presented by Maskelyne and became a feature in Bess and Harry Houdini's first show in the early days of his career. For this illusion the magician is handcuffed and placed inside a sack, then locked in a trunk. His assistant stands on top of the trunk. As she raises a curtain, she is instantly changed into the magician. The magician then opens the trunk and there is the assistant, handcuffed and inside the sack.

Variations possible within each of the types of large-scale illusions are endless. Assistants appear in boxes or tanks of water or locked in trunks or cabinets. Anything can be made to disappear, including horses and riders, pianos, automobiles, even the magicians themselves. (Several attempts have been made to cause an elephant to vanish. Houdini was successful on stage in New York. Less successful were Howard Thurston, whose elephant died, and Harry Blackstone, whose elephant was too temperamental to walk on creaking stages.) Women can be vivisected in various ways: face down or face up; in thirds, halves, or quarters; crosswise or longitudinally, humorously or maniacally. Men change to women, women to animals, animals to men. Anything can float in the air from a car to a camel caravan.

In large stage shows, each illusion generally had special scenery and costuming with some smaller effects built around it. A full-evening show would resemble a series of playlets, each with an illusion as the finale. Today such spectacles are seen on television, and in recent years several musical comedies devoted entirely to magic have appeared. Large-scale illusions are also sometimes used in short sequences or as the spectacular climax of a cabaret show.

However arranged, a successful large-scale illusion depends equally on the quality of the presentation and on the construction of the equipment. If an illusion is to be used in a cabaret act, it often is designed and built by the magician who presents it. In other cases, a magician may take his idea to a designer like John Gaughn, Eric Lewis, Les Smith, or Robert Harbin, who specializes in building magic equipment. These men work with the magician to refine an idea or engineer a design so the illusion can be realized on stage. According to such experts, there are no new principles in magic. Eric Lewis says, "There are only seeds."

The development of equipment for a first-rate illusion results from the skillful use of an old discovery plus a novel approach to current informa-

tion. But the equipment is only half the job. Once the equipment has been successfully built, the illusion must be well presented. "It takes a clever person to be able to pull these things off," says John Gaughn. "If people see a good magician materialize a girl in a box, they will say, 'Where did she come from?' But if they see a bad magician do the same trick, they will only find the box clever. A good magician is much more than someone who just pushes boxes around on the stage."

A magician doesn't push boxes around on stage, he creates mystery around boxes. It is sometimes contended that any competent actor could present a large-scale illusion. Perhaps so, but it would take a competent magician to train the actor; so the point is lost. Bautier de Kolta's Vanishing Lady is a good example. Although the illusion has been presented by many magicians since de Kolta first performed it, no one else has been successful in making both the girl and the silk vanish. To make both disappear requires a complicated series of preliminary movements that must be masked from the audience. The choreography of the trick has proved too difficult for other magicians to master.

In order to conceive, build, and present such an illusion, the conjurer and all whom he employs must be able to see the entire trick as a single unit. They must know the view the audience will have. They must never forget how the equipment will look before and after the illusion is completed, how it will move and how it will be handled.

Harry Kellar, who based his reputation as a magician on large-scale illusions, said, "Your art can never arrive at the perfection of art until your handling of the illusion produces a thrill of genuine surprise in all who behold it." When a master magician presents a grand illusion, it is forever stamped with his personality. Another performer may present the trick, but he cannot duplicate its magic. Great illusionists like Kellar, Maskelyne, and Alexander Herrmann found it unnecessary to place the word magician on their handbills; anyone catching sight of one of the names knew immediately who he was. Like the image the Wizard of Oz cast on a screen, the illusionist enlarges himself to command his stage. At a wave of his hand, objects rise into the air. At the crack of his pistol, humans disappear in a puff of smoke.

THURSTON

I f any magician evokes the great Wizard of Oz, it is Howard Thurston. He billed his magic show (the largest and most opulent the world has seen) as *The Wonder Show of the Universe.* Named as Harry Kellar's successor in 1908, Thurston went on to expand Kellar's show to over three times its original size. Thurston presented 18 instead of five large-scale illusions, hauled three railroad cars full of equipment, and employed 40 assistants. He made a million dollars from his magic but lost most of it through bad investments. After his death, his equipment was sold for a pittance. But he lived well through a colorful career, performed for royalty all over the world, and was the first magician to present a show on Broadway. "Always make sure they spell your name right" was one cogent remark attributed to Thurston. "Never believe your own publicity" was another.

Thurston did not aspire to a life of magic, although as a boy of seven he was impressed by a

Thurston was a small man and very handsome. He was known for the dignity he maintained on stage.

performance of Herrmann the Great in Columbus, Ohio. The son of a midwestern carriage maker, Thurston worked hard as a child, beginning as a bellboy at the age of nine. At twelve he was a newsboy. While hawking papers, Thurston met a jockey not much older than he was and ran away with him to Cincinnati. Parting company with the jockey, Thurston wandered on alone. He worked as an exercise boy at race tracks or peddled papers as he roamed from city to city. By fourteen Thurston was doing magic tricks in the streets, and at sixteen returned home a prodigal son. Perhaps bored at home after his free-wheeling existence, he amused himself with sleight of hand.

In 1886, at seventeen, Thurston met a Mr. Round and acquired religion. He soon found himself preaching on street corners. He was sufficiently persuasive to impress Mrs. E. E. Thomas, one of Round's supporters. Mrs. Thomas was a wealthy woman, and she decided to provide Thurston with an education. He was sent to the Moody School at Mt. Hermon, Massachusetts, to prepare for a career as a medical missionary. On Christmas night, 1887, Thurston presented his first formal magic performance for his schoolmates.

In 1892, after four years at the Moody school and 18 months helping on a farm for delinquent boys, Thurston was en route to the University of Philadelphia when he caught sight of a poster advertising Herrmann the Great. Remembering his childhood delight at the great magician's performance, Thurston decided to see the show. Afterward the young man was suddenly torn between the glamorous life of a magician and the zealous fervor of missionary work. The next morning Thurston was purchasing a ticket to Philadelphia when he saw Alexander and Adelaide Herrmann boarding a train for Syracuse. Thurston looked at the ticket in his hand. It, too, was for Syracuse. Without further debate, he boarded the train. Though Thurston never spoke to the Herrmanns during the trip to Syracuse, he had cast his lot with magic. Missionary work was out of the question.

Thurston traveled to Michigan where he performed magic and sold potato peelers. In Cleveland, he joined the Sells Brothers Circus and became the magician in the Great London Sideshow. They had only one banner—so Thurston worked as Anderson, the Great Wizard of the North. On his own in Boulder, Colorado, in 1896, Thurston developed the trick which was to make him famous. The Rising Cards effect had always been done by holding the deck in a goblet while the chosen card popped up. Thurston held the deck in his hand, then was inspired to make the selected card float from the pack and soar above his head. Not long after, Thurston was performing in a small variety show in Denver at the same time that Leon Herrmann, nephew of the great Alexander, was appearing in a larger hall. Thurston rushed to show Herrmann his new version of the Rising Cards. Herrmann admitted he had been fooled and offered to buy the trick. Thurston declined to sell it, but urged a witnessing newspaperman (Thurston had brought him along) to report the incident in the *Denver Post*. Thereafter, Thurston

could bill himself as "The Man who Mystified Herrmann."

Tired of wandering in wagons, playing in small theaters, dime museums, and sideshows, Thurston went to New York in 1899. The audacious young man pushed his way into an agent's office and supplied his own prepaid audience to applaud while he auditioned. The agent was impressed and Thurston embarked on a nationwide tour.

Thurston amazed audiences throughout the United States, not only with his Rising Cards effect, but with his skill at sailing cards to any location in the theater. Resplendent in white formal attire, he began each performance by pitching a deck of cards to the audience. When he dexterously manipulated cards, he worked with his arms bared to the elbows. Thurston was known for his great dignity on stage, but humor was also a part of every performance. One of his favorite tricks was to pull a quacking duck from beneath the

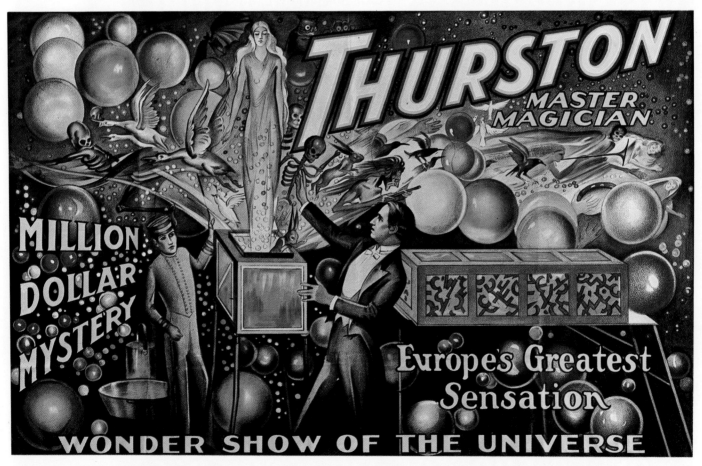

Like many magicians starting early in this century, Thurston found Europe to be more receptive to magicians than America. In London he fashioned an elaborate show with which he toured the continent and eventually the United States.

In the Iasia Illusion, a girl in a cage was lifted above the heads of the audience. After curtains surrounded the cage, she threw souvenir cards from a slit in the fabric until Thurston fired a pistol. At the gunshot the side curtains fell and the cage bottom dropped. The girl had vanished.

coat of a surprised member of the audience.

In 1900 he received a contract to play the Princess Theatre in London. His four-week engagement was extended to six months, and then he toured the continent. He was personally congratulated by the Prince of Wales, gave a command performance for the shah of Iran, and received a gold watch from Emperor Franz Josef of Austria.

Not a man to rest on his laurels, Thurston returned to London to fashion a huge illusion show. He worked on it for nine months, then rented the Princess Theatre for his opening engagement. He replaced his white tuxedo with the costume of an oriental prince, including a silk turban, riding breeches, and high leather boots. Electric fountains and bowls of colored fire decorated the stage. He performed the Floating Ball illusion in which he levitated a golden sphere.

He turned a statue into a living woman, then made her vanish under a silk. Women flashed mysteriously into view on pedestals. At the show's climax this storybook magician stood on stage with water pouring endlessly from his right hand and fire leaping from his left. As was his custom, each performance began with his famous Rising Cards and astoundingly accurate Card Pitching. Critics were enthralled, and he was booked for a tour of the United States.

But Thurston's career was only beginning. Restless and full of energy, he was constantly adding new illusions. In 1905, he sailed to Australia. He arrived without money and was unable to redeem his equipment from a port warehouse. Again audacity determined his fate. He sold Franz Josef's gold watch for four gold pieces, then successfully palmed himself off as a rich American magician. He found a backer and his tour in Australia became a profitable venture.

After Australia, Thurston toured the Philippines, China, Japan, Java, Burma, and India. He performed in a specially made tent in Benares, India, pointedly ignoring an outbreak of cholera. He had Indian conjurers to entertain him while he relaxed in bed with morning coffee. Learning that Harry Kellar was about to choose a successor, Thurston rushed back to the United States. Thurston spent one year performing with the older

magician before Kellar formally declared him his successor. Thurston retained Kellar's levitation illusion and spirit cabinet but introduced new illusions for the remainder of the production.

Thurston was beginning all over again. "The thing I had won by endless effort," he wrote, "was consuming me with grief—not so much because of debts and accompanying troubles, but the possibility of failure that lurked at every turn." The show continued to increase in size. He improved Kellar's levitation of Princess Karnac by inviting members of the audience on stage to verify the feat. Witnesses reported that the suspense Thurston created was so powerful the audience was convinced that any noise would send the floating princess crashing to the floor. He was able to hold viewers transfixed for up to ten minutes.

Each year Thurston added new illusions to his lavish production. He presented a Vanishing Piano illusion in which a young woman playing a piano was hoisted into the air and vanished. A woman performing equestrian feats atop a white Arabian horse mounted a platform and disappeared, horse and all. Similarly, a Whippet automobile full of female assistants vanished in a puff of smoke.

In 1919 Thurston made magic history when he brought his show to Broadway. During the finale, water gushed from everything he touched with his magic wand. By 1923 there was enough demand for Thurston's magic so that he owned three road companies as well as his own show. He finished his autobiography, *My Life of Magic*, in 1929 and also produced a mystery play entitled *The Demon*. Thurston first announced his retirement in 1931, then again in 1934. In between he was featured on his own radio show twice a week. Howard Thurston died while on tour in the spring of 1936 after suffering a paralytic stroke.

Thurston was a great flim-flam man, a bold adventurer, and a master magician. Married four times, the last at the age of sixty-five, he toured the world during a life of tempestuous ups and downs. His autobiography is a sparkling chronicle. "Long experience has taught me that the crux of my fortunes is whether I can radiate good will toward the audience," he concludes. "There is only one way to do it and that is to feel it. You can fool the eyes and the minds of the audience, but you cannot fool their hearts."

CHUNG LING SOO

Eastern magic did not make its debut in the Western world until the nineteenth century. Troupes of Indian, Chinese, and Japanese conjurers had performed earlier in England, but rarely was a single performer featured. The first Chinese magician to achieve prominence in the Western world was named Ching Ling Foo. (His American imitator, who took the name Chung Ling Soo, became even more famous.) Billed as "Conjurer to the Empress of China," Ching Ling Foo won the admiration of American and European audiences when he toured in 1898. His most spectacular illusion was his version of the Goldfish Bowl effect. Dressed in flowing Chinese robes, he exhibited both sides of a cloth to his audience. He lowered it to the floor, then flung it aside to reveal a huge porcelain bowl, filled with water and floating red apples. Soon Chinese conjurers were the rage in both the United States and Europe.

The American imitator who became even more famous than the original was William Ellsworth Robinson. Before assuming an Eastern aspect, Robinson had credentials in the magic world. Born in New York in 1861, he first performed magic at the age of fourteen. He became builder and assistant in the companies of Kellar, Alexander Herrmann, and Leon Herrmann.

In 1900, an agent offered Robinson work in Paris if he could duplicate Ching Ling Foo's act. Robinson accepted the offer. With a Chinese conjurer, he performed in Paris and then in England, where he first used the name he was to keep the rest of his life, Chung Ling Soo. In time, Robinson acted an oriental role both on and off stage.

At first, as Chung Ling Soo, Robinson duplicated his counterpart's routines almost exactly, but he did not limit himself to mere imitation. He was innovative and worked constantly to improve his show. Many of his effects were immensely complicated. Often they ended with the appearance of his wife, Suee Seen. He was known to pull her from a pot of boiling water, materialize her in a display of huge dice, shoot an arrow through her, and make her appear in an enlarged oyster shell. He produced doves from bran and yards of colored streamers from his mouth. In an aerial fishing effect, he cast a line into the audience and reeled it in with four live goldfish. Once, Chung Ling Soo and the original Ching Ling Foo played opposite each other in London theaters. The American outpulled his Chinese counterpart.

But Chung Ling Soo's name is indelible in the annals of magic not because of his elaborate performances but due to the circumstances of his death. His most dramatic illusion was his death-

After William Ellsworth Robinson began appearing as the oriental magician Chung Ling Soo, he no longer acknowledged his occidental birth. It is said he even gave interviews through a Chinese interpreter.

defying Bullet Catch. Like Alexander Herrmann before him, Chung Ling Soo used a china plate to catch bullets fired at him from an old-fashioned musket. On March 23, 1918, his London show ended in tragedy. Brandishing a china plate while two assistants fired at his heart, Chung Ling Soo suddenly cried out and dropped to the stage. By morning William Ellsworth Robinson was dead. Rumor and suspicion surrounded the event, and a Scotland Yard investigation ensued. Chung Ling Soo was not the first magician to die as a result of the feat. In 1830, an Indian performer in London was killed while enacting the Bullet Catch, and in an earlier performance of the stunt, one Phillip Astley shot his wife.

Chung Ling Soo assumed these elaborate grimaces during his Fire Trick. He remained mute throughout his performances and became a master at the art of mime.

This complicated illusion began when Chung Ling Soo boiled a great cauldron of water. From the steaming pot, he produced flocks of live ducks, rabbits, and his wife, Suee Seen.

Some of the finest lithographs in magic advertising were made for Chung Ling Soo. This one may be somewhat presumptuous considering Soo was not Chinese.

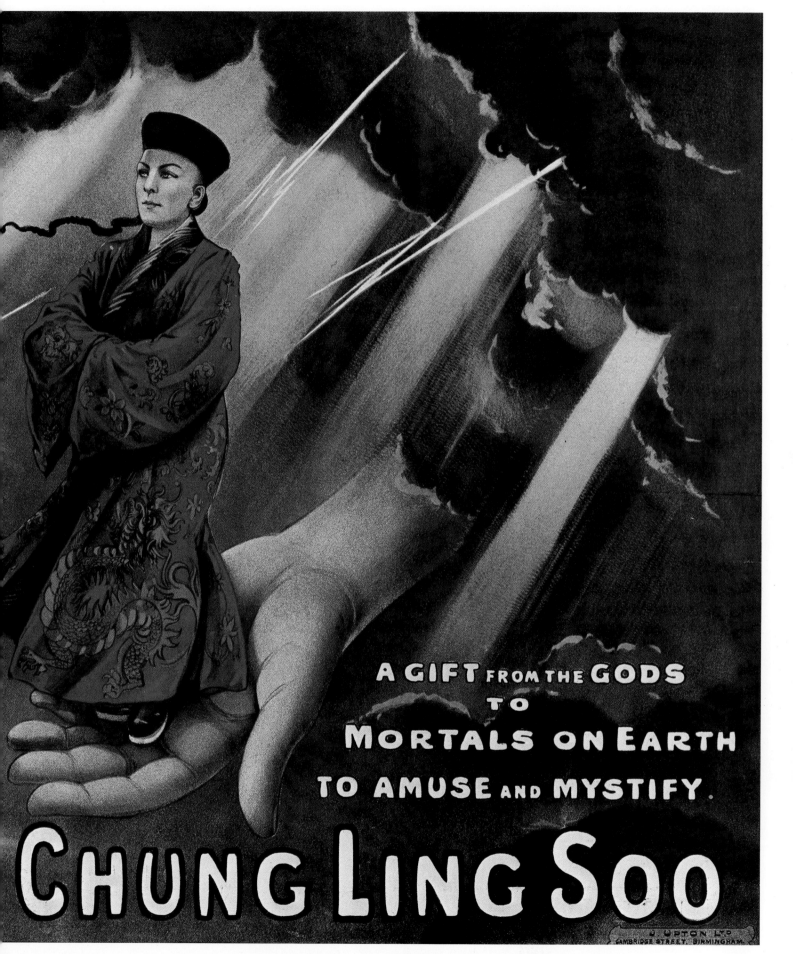

This simple but striking poster for Harry Blackstone's act was unusual for the flamboyant era, particularly among magicians.

BLACKSTONE

In 1917, at the age of twenty-two, Harry Blackstone was not only firmly established in vaudeville but had developed his own two-hour road show. The young magician already offered strong competition for both Thurston and Dante (the head of Thurston's second road company). After Dante moved to Europe in 1927 to avoid competition with Thurston, and Thurston retired in 1931, the field was clear for Blackstone. He quickly moved to the top of his profession in the United States.

In comparison with the devilish Dante and the dignified Thurston, Blackstone was a flamboyant cowboy on stage. He always performed the most strenuous illusions himself. In one sequence, his roguish assistants succeeded in subduing a struggling Blackstone, tying him up and stuffing him into a sack which was then hoisted high in the air. Within seconds a horseman thundered on stage and fired a pistol. At the sound of the gunshot, the sack dropped, empty, and the rider revealed himself as Blackstone. At the end of the sequence he and his white horse both disappeared. Sometimes, for variety, only the horse vanished, leaving a seemingly mystified magician behind.

Blackstone's show included a Vanishing Horse, Vanishing Auto, and Vanishing Camel. The balky camel proved difficult. Not only did he refuse to cooperate, but his health was not the best and he died. Blackstone's Dancing Handkerchief, however, brought him more enduring fame than any of the spectacular illusions that headlined his production. He began the effect by borrowing a handkerchief from someone in the audience. As soon as he tied a knot in one corner, the innocuous bit of cloth appeared to become an animated being. It danced in time with music, wriggled when it was tickled, and displayed a personality and will of its own. The instant the handkerchief was untied, all evidence of enchantment ceased.

No one since has duplicated Blackstone's success with the Dancing Handkerchief. But his son, Harry Blackstone Jr., offers a version of his father's famous Vanishing Birdcage. Blackstone Jr. holds a small birdcage complete with canary in front of his body. Witnesses on stage place their hands on the cage. In spite of these precautions, cage and bird are gone in the flick of an eye.

Blackstone was famous for his thick crop of wavy hair and deep resonant voice.

An outdoor crowd watches Blackstone perform a challenge escape from a packing crate. He often used such stunts for publicity.

SHIMADA

Haruo Shimada's magic is pure artistry. His routines are the quintessence of choreography—colorful as a handful of silks, graceful as a dance, and so beautiful the audience is transfixed. Whether producing doves in a Western setting, doing his parasol routine in Japanese surroundings, or presenting his spectacular Dragon Illusion, Shimada is worth watching again and again.

For Shimada, magic is all-encompassing. From the age of thirteen he devoted himself to the art. At first, he attended night classes in Tokyo and worked at magic counters of department stores in the daytime. One day, while demonstrating magic tricks, he was complimented on his technique with billiard balls. Shimada immediately apprenticed himself to a professional Japanese magician. "The only way to become a professional magician in Japan is to be the student of a professional," he says. "I became a student and dropped almost everything else. I spent five years with my teacher Tenyo. I traveled the country with him. I packed the illusions, assisted him on stage and sometimes performed myself. I produced 35 billiard balls in my routine—and called it Millionball. But it was a very hard time. Hardly any amateur magicians were traveling in the country."

At eighteen, Shimada left Tenyo to become a professional conjurer. Tenyo was doing a dove production at the time, and Shimada adapted the techniques to create his own version. By chance he happened to see a Channing Pollock film. "Every young magician has an idol," says Shimada. "I wanted to be like Channing. And I did well with doves in the cabarets of Japan. There weren't many dove acts there."

A few years later, Shimada traveled to Australia with a Japanese company of variety acts. At a theater in Adelaide he met his future wife and assistant, Deanna. He spoke no English and she no Japanese. His contract stipulated that he was to return to Japan at the conclusion of the tour. He did, but he went back to Australia four months later. Shimada was given a contract to perform at a

nightclub in Sydney, and Deanna became his assistant. They were in love, and Shimada's working papers were not quite in order. They quickly married without telling their parents.

Haruo and Deanna Shimada worked three years in Australia. During an engagement in Sydney, they met a Mexican couple and were offered a contract to appear at the largest variety theater in Mexico City. They toured Mexico, returned to Japan, and then toured the Orient. Next, they ventured to Europe. Shimada still wanted to emulate Channing Pollock, but he found the continental market glutted with dove acts.

---

1. A magic dragon has entrapped Shimada (wearing a Kabuki mask) within its long, sinuous body.

---

2. Shimada slays the mythical beast; then he and Deanna burst unexpectedly from its body.

Shimada was obstinate; it had to be doves. In London times were hard for the couple and their daughter. Shimada was unable even to get an audition. No one was interested in an oriental magician who produced doves.

They returned to Mexico, where Shimada's dove act was popular, and signed a contract for a weekly television show. "We were famous in Mexico," says Shimada. "People knew us when we walked down the street. But I wanted to be successful in Europe and America."

To succeed, Shimada gave up his cherished dream temporarily. Dove acts were simply unsalable. In Mexico, Shimada and Deanna began to work on a parasol routine. Ironically Shimada, unable to find work with a Western style, became the

103

2. Shimada is disguised in a Kabuki mask. With lyrical movements he dances across the stage.

3. As Shimada dances, Deanna pulls yards and yards of colorful silks knotted together from his mouth.

1. Shimada makes a golden fan appear. He dances with it, holds it high above his head, then lowers it to cover his face.

first oriental magician since Ching Ling Foo to achieve prominence with oriental wizardry. In creating his parasol effects, he drew on magic traditions of his own heritage. "The parasols," says Shimada, "originally come from China. They have been used magically for more than 200 years, but always in the same style. The standard performance is done with a lot of silk handkerchiefs. Parasols are produced closed from the silks, then opened and placed on the floor. I was the first magician to produce parasols with sleight-of-hand techniques, and the first to produce open parasols."

When Shimada produces parasols, they burst forth in an incredible show of color. "Oh," marveled one onlooker, "he pulls them out of the air, out of his ears, from everywhere." Shimada stretches a hand and a green parasol pops open in it. He shakes

a piece of thin, black tissue paper and it is transformed into a large black parasol. Parasols of all colors and sizes blossom everywhere. "Shimada," commented one magician, "does as many effects in 15 minutes as most magicians do in 45."

Shimada is charismatic on stage. Dai Vernon once remarked that a magician needs sex appeal, and Shimada certainly has that. His hands are expressive, and his stylized motions are those of a dancer. Yet his face and figure are strong, invoking images of the legendary samurai warriors. He dresses in the courtly attire of a Japanese gentleman, while Deanna wears an abbreviated kimono. Behind them, lavish scenery of painted cherry blossoms recalls a Madame Butterfly setting. Accompanying the performance is traditional Japanese music, arranged to suit Western tastes and to

4. Shimada removes the mask and draws the last of the scarves from the mask himself. A tiny red-and-white parasol pops out with the last scarf. Smiling broadly, Shimada opens it and spins it in his fingers to the delight of the audience.

help them time the performance. "You lose the act's tempo if you go too heavily into cultural music," says Shimada. "But we use classical Japanese music and have kept it as close as possible to the original." Shimada and Deanna move with precision as parasol after parasol appears, flaming torches turn into fiery umbrellas, and flowers plucked from Deanna's hair seem to multiply endlessly in Shimada's fingers.

The Shimadas first presented the parasol act on stage at the 1970 *It's Magic* show in Los Angeles, produced by Milt Larsen. After presenting the routine for about five years, they returned to Japan to fashion their Dragon Illusion as a spectacular finish for the act. It was first presented at the *It's Magic* show in 1975. Shimada drew from traditional Japanese folk dances and myths in creating

this illusion. The dragon character occurs in the mythology of both the Japanese and the Chinese. Ryujin, the Dragon King of the Sea, was one of the primal Japanese deities. Jimmu Tenno, the legendary Japanese emperor, was the son of one of the Dragon King's daughters, Princess Jewel-Good, and the great-great-grandson of Amaterasu, the Goddess of the Sun. "Magic," says Shimada, "is fantasy, and folk tales have been a source of beautiful fantasy for centuries."

The Dragon Illusion is a transposition, but the entire sequence is drawn from Japanese sources. First, Shimada dances in and out of his flower-blossom scenery and by turning the panels to mirrors, alters the mood on the stage. Then, he dances with a magical sword that floats horizontally from the palm of his hand. According to myths

1. Magic parasol blossoms open like exotic flowers under the control of Shimada's wonderful hands.

2. Hardly has one parasol appeared in Shimada's left hand when another equally colorful blooms in his right.

1. Shimada steps forward on the stage at the beginning of his dove act and his black cane mysteriously bursts into flame.

2. He removes one of his white gloves and lets it rest lightly on his outstretched palm.

3. Shimada turns the glove over in his hand with the simplest and most casual of gestures.

4. The glove instantly changes into a white dove. The impact of the fluttering bird in the somber setting is electric.

of the Japanese, the mirror, the sword, and the jewel were gifts presented by the gods to the Imperial house of Japan. Shimada exchanges his sword for a spear and continues his theatrical war dance until a resplendent dragon bursts onto the stage. Shimada fights the dragon. As Shimada disappears within the folds of the dragon's body, the beast dies with a last fiery gasp. In the flurry of the creature's demise, Deanna and Shimada leap from its body to bow to well-deserved applause.

Although Shimada's reputation is now built on the parasol act, he has not abandoned his doves. He is considered one of the foremost dove manipulators in the world, and since Channing Pollock's retirement, many feel that Shimada has assumed his place. Pollock's influence is visible in Shimada's work, not so much in style but in mood. Shimada also uses white doves, black clothing, and red silks to create a dark and sensuous atmosphere. He wears the traditional attire of a Western magician: he enters wearing a tuxedo, gloved and carrying a black cane. But because he is Japanese, Shimada does not fit any stereotype. His appearance is immediately arresting, a sensation accentuated by Deanna's Western beauty. She is regal in a long black dress and glittering tiara, earrings, and necklace. The two might be on their way to an elegant, fashionable evening event.

Shimada's technique in handling his doves is quite different from Pollock's though his mood is also romantic. Pollock seemed almost to sculpt doves in his hands; when Shimada produces doves they pop spontaneously into view. He fans a deck of cards with brightly hued backs and presto: there is a white dove perched on top. He extends his cane and instantly a dove flutters into sight. Shimada throws a dove into the air, and instead of flapping wings, a white silk floats slowly to the stage.

When the situation seems right, Shimada presents the dove act. It is more portable and not as space demanding as the parasols and the dragon. But Shimada's oriental routines suit him better. He seems more comfortable in his Japanese clothing, and his movements seem freer and more fluid. The setting increases the scope of his presentation, allowing him to use his personal history and the history of his land. "Japanese who think that the Western way is the modern way are losing their character," he says.

Perhaps more important, the parasols and the dragon are unique. With these routines, Shimada presents magic that only he can perform successfully. "Somebody has to try something new," he says. "You can't say who is the best magician because everybody can be best in his own way. But becoming commercially successful—that's another thing. If I could have things just as I wanted them, I would like to work in Las Vegas. To be a success there, a magic act has to be as strong as any other kind of act.

"Physically our routine would be very hard to perform six days a week, several times a day. But in many ways it would be ideal. It would give us an opportunity to learn and to polish."

In the finale of his parasol routine, Shimada whirls amid a bright downpour of confetti.

MARK WILSON

ark Wilson's career in magic differs from that of most magicians. Although he has performed in night clubs, stage shows, and other live presentations throughout the country, Wilson prefers to work in television. Most people, magicians and producers alike, consider television to be a difficult medium for magic. "When I first proposed a television program devoted to magic," says Wilson, "the television experts questioned three things. First, they thought viewers would think the magic was done with trick photography. Second, they felt magic would only be enjoyed by children. And third, they said, 'That's fine, but what are you going to do for your second show?' None of them realized the variety that magic has." Television producers have become aware of the potential of magic on the TV screen, and Mark Wilson is one of the reasons why. His network television show, *The Magic Land of Alakazam,* the first show of its kind, ran for five years. As magic increased in popularity, Wilson continued to produce specials and to act as a guest star on variety shows. Wilson was successful in these endeavors through his personal promotional skills and because he understood what changes would be necessary to adapt the art form to TV.

Wilson wanted to be a magician early in his life. "My father was a traveling salesman," he says. "We traveled so much I was brought up in hotels. I played in the lobbies. The first time I saw a professional magician I was eight years old. We were in Indianapolis. We went to the movies and there were stage acts between the features. Tommy Windsor produced fans of cards, silver dollars, and a wine glass full of wine. I remember every detail of his act. On the way to Dallas (we finally settled in Dallas and I was raised there) I bought Thurston's *Fifty New Card Tricks.* It showed me how to produce cards from the air. That was the first trick I learned.

1. In the Penetrating Glass Illusion, Wilson demonstrates that the glass is solid by rapping it sharply.

2. Still striking the glass, Wilson attaches targets to both sides of the panel.

"I used to spend my allowance for magic props. In 1942, when I was fifteen, I began working at the Douglas Magic Shop in Dallas. I demonstrated magic. I worked every day. Whenever I wasn't in school I was at the magic shop. They started me at $2.50 a day and in six months doubled my salary.

"I wanted to be a professional magician, but I also wanted to be a financial success. I could see that often people working in magic were not earning much. It seemed to me that I could channel a career so I could be successful and still be doing what I wanted to do. I went to Southern Methodist University and majored in advertising. My object was to adapt magic to advertising and sales promotion, so magic could be used to move merchandise.

"While I was still in school, I sold the idea to the Morton Potato Chip Company. If you had a group of 35 people or more, you could call Morton and the company would send me to perform. It didn't cost anything. I was paid by Morton. I used to do 30 to 80 half-hour shows a month. During that time I acquired the background I needed to work full time as a professional magician."

After Wilson finished school, he took his magic expertise and sales know-how to the Dr. Pepper Bottling Company in Waco, Texas. He sold them a local television show which became the highest rated afternoon show on the air in Waco, even outranking network competition.

When Mark married his wife, Nani, they presented TV magic shows as a team in Dallas, Houston, and San Antonio. Money was tight and video tape was not yet perfected. The two spent most of their time driving from one city to another. During this period, Wilson worked out a prospectus for a network magic show.

"I didn't know how hard it was for an individual to sell a network show," he says. "It took me two years to do it. In 1958 I started making calls. I would save some money and call on every advertising agency and prospective client I could think of. Cereal, candy, toys, everybody. In 1959, I sold a syndicated series to the 3M Company located in Minneapolis. We called the show *The Magic Circus* It was aired in six cities during a 15-week test." But three shows were being considered for the

3. Wilson slides Nani through the sheet of glass. Though her body passes easily through the glass, when the targets are removed, it is as solid as before the penetration.

available time period, and *The Magic Circus* wasn't chosen.

"It was quite a blow," says Wilson. "I had worked a long time to get to that point. But I started selling again. When I have something that's good and I'm sold on it and it's right, if someone doesn't buy it, I don't get discouraged. I tell myself I must have done something wrong or they would have bought it. I work on it some more and try to sell it to someone else." In 1960, the Kellogg Company bought Wilson's program.

Wilson successfully adapted magic to fit the constraints of the TV medium and captivated children and adults across the country. When Mark and Nani Wilson performed, magic became fun. Both have pleasing personalities and do not strain to entertain. They work as a team, now sometimes assisted by their son, Greg. As an assistant, Nani is always good-humored, whether she is being levitated, sawn in half, or made to appear in a tank of water. On stage, the Wilsons have the homey, family feeling of being just folks.

The warmth the couple generates overcomes the objections most magicians feel towards TV. In general, conjurers contend that TV is a "cold" medium, in the sense that they feel distant from the audience and that a live performance does not come across well on the small screen. Mark and Nani Wilson owe a good measure of their TV success to the fact that they do not attempt a heavily dramatic portrayal of magic. Their magic is brightly illuminated; it is performed as if by the light of day. They maintain a consistent brightness of tone. Their illusions are surprising, exciting, and enjoyable but they are not awesome or eerie.

The Wilsons' seemingly effortless performance is the summation of years of practice. Wilson choreographs his magic carefully. Each illusion progresses simply and logically. What happens in each trick is readily evident to the audience. Large-scale illusionists of the past sometimes used such complicated productions that the final outcome was somewhat murky, but Wilson designs illusions that are straightforward in both concept and presentation.

Wilson is assisted by experts. He employed a staff of 17 during the television series. "I always

1. Mark Wilson asks his wife and assistant, the beautiful Nani Darnell, to enter the Train Illusion.

had five to ten magicians on staff," he says. "We would sit around together and brainstorm. We made 99 different 30-minute shows for *The Magic Land of Alakazam.*"

Wilson's magic is also well suited to the needs of industrial trade shows. After his television series was concluded, he concentrated on industrial-show devices. "From 1963 to 1970," he says, "I worked largely with trade shows. I had offices in New York, Chicago, and Los Angeles. Four or five shows would be going on at the same time. And we did shows for most of the major state fairs in the United States at one time or another.

"Trade shows are put together a little differently. The object is to create effects that can be presented without your actually being there. When I got into trade shows, I started taking out patents. Few magicians want patents for their designs because when you take out a patent, you expose the trick to the world. I am one of the few who believe patents are worthwhile. To date I have five on my illusions."

In 1971 Wilson moved back into television. He put together a series of one hour specials for Pillsbury. These shows were also titled *The Magic Circus.* His contract was for six shows to be presented over the course of four years, and they have been sold internationally in a number of countries, including Sweden, Brazil, and the Philippines.

Wilson has expanded his magic in many directions. He also has animated corporate symbols for television and has created magic shows for amuse-

2. Smiling and wriggling her fingers and toes, Nani hardly seems disturbed by the metal blade Wilson pushes through her.

3. Nani continues to move her hands and feet as Wilson slides the front half of the train forward along the track.

4. Exuberant, Wilson jumps through the separated halves of the train to prove they are disconnected. The still-smiling Nani remains calm. This illusion, the only one of its kind, is a Mark Wilson original.

ment parks. He began by creating the Hall of Magic for General Cigar at the 1965 New York World's Fair. There, he supplied the illusions and narrated the action but did not actually perform.

Wilson has also produced magic shows for Hershey Park in Pennsylvania, Astro World in Texas, and Bush Gardens in California. "But we are not in the business of selling complete presentations," says Wilson. "We don't sell the magic; we only supply and perform it."

In order to carry out his many ambitious projects, Wilson employs a large staff at his offices in Los Angeles, including clerical personnel, photographers, builders, carpenters, and designers. He still has several other magicians available, and they are often called upon to serve as magic consultants. For example, his staff assisted the Australian road company of *The Magic Show* and designed magic for a Cat Stevens production.

By televising his magic, Wilson introduced thousands of people to the art. For him, magic is both a performance and a business, but the two are not at odds. "People are finally beginning to realize that magic isn't just for children," he says. "Perhaps one day they will see that it has even more appeal to adults." Wilson realized his personal goals, advanced the profession, and created room for new talent. Not since the early part of the century has magic functioned on such a broad basis.

5. Wilson disengages the track and reverses Nani's two halves. She continues to wave her hands and flex her feet.

6. Wilson restores Nani as easily as he divided her. He assists her, whole once again, to climb from the train.

DAVID COPPERFIELD

orn in 1956, David Copperfield is the youngest professional magician in this volume. He augments his magic with dance and drama; conjuring and the theater are his abiding passions. Copperfield believes that magic, whether close-up conjuring or large-scale illusions, can be strong only if it has equal parts of magical skill and good theater. "Sleight of hand and an ability to handle large props," he says, "are necessary for the performance of fine magic. But the presentation must be as polished and calculated as the trick itself. It is

1. After they have danced a duet, David Copperfield entrances his assistant, Cheryl Pallas. He helps her to lie on the couch and places his magic wand in her folded hands.

2. Copperfield makes mysterious passes in the air above Cheryl, compelling her body to rise from the couch. He motions upward, and at his command she begins to float in the air.

3. As the couch is moved offstage, Cheryl rises slowly and dramatically into the air. With his powerful hands, Copperfield seems to control every movement of the young woman's body.

4. At the end of the illusion, Cheryl is floating so high in the air that Copperfield must stand on a small ladder in order to pass a hoop over her body. Beginning at her feet, he moves the hoop along her body and over her head.

as important as the illusion. Magic has direction when it has setting, mood, and style. Too often the theatrical potential of magic has been overlooked in favor of the illusion. The illusion gets the applause instead of the magician. I want to add something to my magic. I'm not satisfied with just doing a trick."

Copperfield, a thin, energetic, dark-eyed young man, is intense and graceful on stage. Each of his illusions becomes a focal point for a dramatic routine featuring music and dance. When he performs a levitation, not only does a young woman float effortlessly in the air, but the magician dances a duet with her. Accompanied by rhapsodic music, she sways with him at the slightest wave of his mesmerizing hand. The dance tells the story. Copperfield as the magician has the power to command the actions of young ladies as well as the force of gravity. The mood, dark and rich, shifts completely when he performs his Strap Escape. Instead of using the dramatic style of most escape artists, Copperfield performs the effect like a lighthearted remake of a Keystone Cops comedy. Bumbling cops try to restrain the magician who dances free repeatedly. Copperfield enjoys adding gaiety to magic. "Magic is a happy thing," he says. "It's supposed to make you happy. Magic needs to have some comedy in it."

Copperfield's style remains frivolous while he presents Backstage with the Magician, an illusion made famous by Dante. The illusion is of the genre known in the trade as a sucker gag. Viewers think they see how a trick is being done but find they have been duped again. Copperfield demonstrates how his assistant can be transferred from one box to another, only to reveal that she has disappeared and someone else has taken her place. Throughout the illusion, Copperfield and his assistants dance about the equipment accompanied by a lighthearted tune.

The mood turns darker when David Copperfield performs his Dancing-Cane effect. His large, expressive hands somehow command the graceful cane in midair. Copperfield not only makes the cane dance, he dances with it. The two are in a fantasy world the audience feels privileged to enter.

The Dancing Cane was the first magic prop to excite Copperfield's imagination. "I started out as a ventriloquist," he says. "One day I was in New York looking for a dummy. I used to visit the magic counters in the department stores. I saw a man doing some simple tricks with a dancing cane. I started taking lessons and put together a birthday-party act with soda bottles and records. I was then twelve years old."

A few years later Copperfield was proficient enough to be asked to give technical assistance to Ben Vereen in a magic sequence of the musical comedy *Pippin*. Copperfield was impressed by Vereen's skill. "There was a black-art thing in *Pippin*," he recalls. "Working on it, I had a chance to see what real theater is like. I always wanted to be like Gene Kelly, but when I saw Ben Vereen's work and what is being done today, the reality and the possibilities, I saw what magic could be." After *Pippin*, Copperfield starred in his own musical magical comedy, *The Magic Man*. His co-star, Cheryl Pallas, remained as his assistant when the play closed after a year-long run in Chicago.

Copperfield designs the costumes for his shows and develops the staging and choreography in his illusions. He finds that adding drama and dance to magic causes complications. The lighting and stage must be properly set to hold the mood of an illusion. "Sometimes I wonder if it is wasteful working out extra things to make an illusion good theater," he says. "I sometimes wonder if all the things I add are detracting from the illusion itself. But I'm going to keep on trying. Part of the problem in presenting magic as theater is in the audience itself. People haven't been exposed to enough magic to tell whether a magician is skilled or unskilled. They don't know how good magic can be.

"I think, though, that the addition of theatricality creates a more lasting impression. The great magicians today are memorable performers, their illusions are strong, their choreography is good, and they are personalities. It's like dance. A dancer learns a dance, but if all he can do are the steps, he stays in the back of the chorus line. To be a star he has to add charisma or theatricality to what he is doing. A good magician creates strong illusions, but he also adds that extra dimension. A good magician is a performer you are glad to see on stage even when he isn't doing magic."

1. In Backstage with the Magician the audience is told it will get a rare look at how an illusion is performed. Copperfield (with his back to us) faces an imaginary audience while we are allowed to see Cheryl hiding behind the red box.

2. After Copperfield has demonstrated that the blue box is empty, we see Cheryl slip into it. Copperfield and his assistant then hoist the empty blue box (only we know that Cheryl is in it) and place it inside the apparently empty red box.

3. Despite our being let in behind the scenes, we have been doubly fooled. Not only does actor Peter Graves come bursting out of the boxes, but Cheryl has disappeared.

1. Doug Henning begins the Mismade Girl illusion by placing his assistant, Michele, inside a multicolored box with four small doors.

2. Henning pushes heavy metal blades into the box, dividing it and, presumably, the girl inside, into four sections.

DOUG HENNING

Doug Henning's magic is young, modern, adventurous in style and setting. Often Henning and his assistants wear simple blue jeans. When not quite so casual, they are decked out in bright satins. Henning's face, framed by long, curling brown hair, is animated and appealing. His voice is soft and sincere. Nothing about his work suggests any other magician.

Henning performs both classic illusions and new ones of his own design. He is one of the most prominent of contemporary magicians and has worked hard and thoughtfully to advance his profession. He believes magic can be a highly poetic dramatic art. Henning deepens his magic, surrounding it with mystery, but he grounds it in a world familiar to his audience.

"When we first see raindrops, as children," he told a group of college students, "it is as wonderful to us as if it were raining emeralds and rubies. After a while we have seen rain so many times we forget how magical it really is. With my magic, I am trying to create that original sense of wonder that the real magic of the world made us feel."

More traditional magicians may lift an eyebrow at an exuberant young man who dashes around the stage wearing tennis shoes, but it is impossible to disparage his success. Henning's Broadway musical, *The Magic Show*, opened in 1974, and was nominated for a Tony award in 1975.

3. In somewhat cavalier fashion, Henning grabs the top section of the box and blithely runs off with it. His assistants follow suit. All three gallop around the stage, spinning and turning with the colorful boxes in their arms.

Several successful road companies toured in various parts of the world. Henning has presented his own live hour-long television special. He has toured the United States, lecturing and performing for packed houses at universities and colleges.

When Henning creates magic, it is fun to watch. In *The Magic Show*, for example, he makes the voluptuous Charmin appear in a glass box. The trick is spectacular. Henning spins a flaming torch, stretches out a hand and in a flash the girl appears in the transparent container. Charmin, however, is not at all pleased. Immediately she begins complaining bitterly that magicians simply will not leave her alone—some wizard or other insists on conjuring her up when she has better things to do. Later, when Henning saws her in half, the illusion becomes the brunt of many jokes. Instead of emphasizing the frightening nature of the effect, Henning spoofs it. Villains (who aren't very villain-

ous) run off with Charmin's lower half before she can be restored. Her upper half is quite distressed.

Yet, the light-hearted humor never interferes with the quality of the illusions. Henning always emphasizes their magical nature. Although he dispensed with heavy dramatics, the audience gulped in suspense when he presented Houdini's famous Water Torture Cell on television. Houdini had emphasized the rigors of his demonstration. Henning did not minimize the danger nor discredit Houdini, but he broke the tension differently. As time ran out and Henning had yet to appear from behind the curtain, the audience could hardly bear to watch. Suddenly, a hooded attendant rushed on stage with an axe to attempt a rescue. Ripping off the hood, the attendant revealed himself as Henning. "I didn't want to come out dripping and coughing," he says. "I thought the illusion would be just as mysterious if I ran onto the stage at the end,

121

4. Henning and his assistants replace the boxes, but they are now in a different order.

disguised as my own rescue man."

Henning's illusions have a quality of mysticism that is charming rather than intimidating. In an illusion he calls Things That Go Bump in the Night, he materializes three great blobs from an empty box. As each miraculously emerges, Henning drapes it in a large, bright silk. The three objects flounder around on the stage until they finally reveal themselves as people. And the thing in the middle is a smiling Doug Henning.

"Good theater helps to motivate magic," says Henning. "When magic becomes more theatrical, it also becomes more magical." His presentation of the Sands of Egypt effect is a case in point. Henning's dramatic treatment makes a simple trick—producing dry sand from a bowl of water—

5. Henning opens the four doors and Michele has been similarly rearranged. She stamps her feet and blows on a noisemaker to prove that she has not suffered inordinately, in spite of her physical reorganization.

seem rich and mysterious. He looks magical and seems to believe in magic himself. Three maidens in flowing robes attend him. The sands are brightly colored reds, yellows, and greens. The actual trick is not as mysterious as its emotional impact. Henning creates mystery with his acting and choreography, as well as with the effect's design.

Henning first saw a performance of magic as a six-year-old child watching television. "I asked my mother what made the woman float in the air. 'Magic,' she said. I still remember the feeling I had. I wanted to be able to create that feeling. I still do.

"Basically, magicians are at four levels. The first might be called a trickster. That's all he does—a trick. 'I fooled you,' he says. Next there is the conjurer. The conjurer not only fools people, he fools them completely. He creates a perfect mystery. But the conjurer adds no poetry, no sense of wonder. The next level of magician—a magician of the first order—adds poetry to the mystery. He works with ordinary objects, and his effects are very beautiful. In the final category is a high order of magician. These can be black or white magicians. A black magician creates mystery in satanic ways, with fiery illusions and strange trappings. A white magician creates wonder and awe in a beautiful way. I am trying to be a white magician. I am trying to create joy with my magic."

Henning's childhood home was in Oakville, Ontario, a suburb of Toronto. He presented his first magic show at fourteen. But after he was graduated from high school, Henning didn't want to pursue a career in magic. "I thought then there were two kinds of magicians," he says, "magicians for kids, and magicians for nightclub acts. I didn't want to be either kind."

So Henning dropped magic and enrolled at McMaster University to study physiological psychology in preparation for pursuing a medical degree. To support himself he worked at Toronto International Airport, loading and unloading crates. Impatient with the heavy work, he decided to try to work his way through school by performing magic. He and a woman friend put together an act called *Henning and Mars* which they presented at local bars and nightclubs.

"I decided to take a couple of years off from school to continue my magic," says Henning. "I applied to the Canada Council for the Arts for a grant

6. Henning and his assistants again run about the stage with the boxes. This time they return them to their original sequence

7. Henning withdraws the blades and opens the box. An undamaged Michele steps triumphantly from the box.

1. In The Microphone Suspension, Henning places Michele in a trance, as she stands upright on a box with her elbow resting on a microphone stand.

2. Henning removes the box, then lifts Michele into a horizontal position. She floats peacefully above the stage, supported only by her elbow.

3. As Michele continues to sleep, suspended four feet in the air, Henning passes a fiery hoop over her body.

in the theater division. I put together a proposal that basically substantiated the equation that magic plus theater equals art. They awarded me a grant of $4,000.

I spent a year traveling around the world, meeting magicians and studying magic. I became a student of Dai Vernon and of Tony Slydini. I decided that it was possible to create art with mystery. I decided I would do magic instead of simply doing tricks. But I discovered there are very few places for a magician to work. I couldn't work in the nightclubs—nightclub acts have to be comedy routines, very fast and sexy. For me that takes away all the artistry. So I worked in coffee houses, then traveled with rock groups. I worked with Canadian bands—Lighthouse and Syrinx. We put together routines combining music and magic. They were so well received I decided to try to create a magic musical.

"With the help of Ivan Reitman and borrowed money, I designed and built some $5,000 worth of illusions. We set up a backer's audition in Toronto. One man saw the potential. He invested $70,000. We composed a score and worked out a plot around the magic, then booked the Royal Alexandra Theatre in Toronto. It took so long to put the show together we had time for only two dress rehearsals, and neither of them were in the theater.

"It took a while for the plot to work. It was hard to work the magic in—we tended to concentrate on illusions and forget about the characters.

1. Doug Henning's Shadow-Box Illusion takes place on a darkened stage. At the outset, his assistants display the empty box.

2. An assistant places a lamp on stage beneath the box. The silhouette of a hand appears; this hand conjures another.

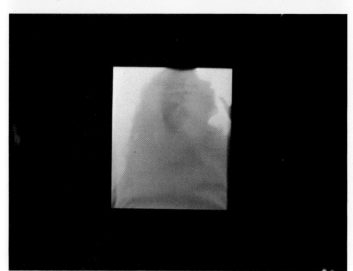

3. The two hands gesture together. Under their influence, the shadow of a face in profile slowly forms.

4. Without warning, a person bursts through the paper and leaps out onto the stage.

But in time it went over. People talked about the show. Eventually *Spellbound* broke every house record at the Royal Alexandra."

Such success was bound to attract attention. Two New York producers, Edgar Lansbury and Joseph Beruh, went to Toronto to see Henning in *Spellbound*. They immediately began trying to convince him to take his show to Broadway. "I didn't want to go to New York," says Henning. "Broadway didn't mean anything to me. Then I met Grover Dale, who became the director of *The Magic Show*. I realized how much I could learn about theater from him; so I decided to go to New York. The magic in *The Magic Show* is the same as it was in *Spellbound*, but we wrote a new story and composed new music. At first we had the same problems as in Toronto. It took a while for the plot

to work. But then it worked and people talked about it and sent their friends to see the show."

His Broadway triumph with *The Magic Show* was a great beginning for Doug Henning. While giving nightly performances in New York, he spent a year developing a live television special that was aired in December, 1975. Henning was given full creative control over the program. He insisted that everything be performed live and that hand-held cameras be used. He created the magic, designed the costumes, and selected the music.

Henning continues to explain the allure of magic and its wonder to audiences that flock to see him at university appearances. "We need more magicians," he says, "but it will take a long time to get them. We have to inspire ten-year-olds now so they will create the fine magic of the future."

5. It is Doug Henning himself, magically materialized inside an empty paper box. The fragility of the structure, glowing with diffused light as the shadowy figure moves within it, creates a peaceful sensation that heightens the surprise of the finish.

SIEGFRIED AND ROY

ometimes performers appear larger-than-life on stage. That is particularly true of Siegfried Fischbacker and Roy Horn. They have an electric magnetism that draws the audience's attention. Their large illusions, featuring a 650-pound tiger, an enormous lion, and a sinuous black panther, are among the most dramatic in the world of magic, and their work is intense and compelling.

Siegfried and Roy are both arresting. Roy is thin, dark haired, and aristocratic; Siegfried is handsome, blond, and strong. Together, they create a mysterious tension. They were the winners of the Las Vegas Entertainment Award for the Most Outstanding Act in show business for four consecutive years, and voted Magicians of the Year in 1976 by over 3,000 of their peers at the Beverly Wilshire Hotel in Los Angeles.

Siegfried and Roy's routine is part of the MGM Grand Hotel's spectacular extravaganza, "Hallelujah Hollywood." The entire show is a Las Vegas version of a lavish Ziegfeld Follies type production featuring dazzling chorus girls, dance ensembles, melodic tenors, and comedians. Siegfried and Roy have the distinction of being the concluding act of the show. In between a dance number and the finale, which features the entire cast, they perform in front of the curtain. In such a limited space the size and power of their illusions is incredible.

The routine begins with Siegfried, dressed in a traditional red-lined cape and black dress suit, performing lightning-fast dove manipulations. The spotlight is on him; the rest of the stage is shrouded in darkness. Despite his light coloring, Siegfried is Mephistophelean, powerful and mysterious. During these quick effects Roy acts as his assistant. The dove manipulations serve two dramatic functions: they establish Siegfried and Roy as magicians, and in case the interest of the audience has slackened during the many preceding acts, they return attention immediately to the stage.

The already fast tempo accelerates when Siegfried and Roy perform their version of Houdini's Metamorphosis. The illusion is so spectacular that even in the hands of less skillful artists it is almost guaranteed to be a crowd pleaser. The orchestra plays the Sabre Dance throughout, increasing the pitch of excitement. As the music begins, the audience, already intrigued by these dazzling performers, is suddenly bolt upright. Roy

1. Siegfried prepares to make Roy disappear. Roy waves farewell to the audience, while Siegfried curtains the cage.

2. Seconds later Leo, a five-year-old African lion weighing some 750 pounds, appears in Roy's place.

3. The mighty cat growls and snarls at Siegfried as he throws open the doors of the cage.

1. Siegfried and Roy's incredible presentation of Houdini's famous Metamorphosis is one of the fastest in the world. The sequence begins as Siegfried locks Roy in silver shackles.

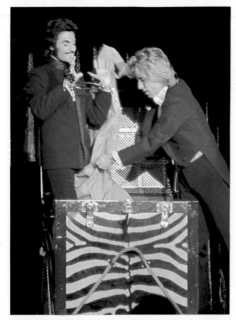

2. Roy steps into the tiger-striped trunk. Siegfried assists him to climb inside a large cloth sack as well.

3. As Roy drops down inside the trunk, Siegfried pulls the sack over his head. He ties up the bag with a cord.

4. After hastily closing and locking the lid, Siegfried quickly ties up the trunk with sturdy rope.

is standing up smiling as Siegfried handcuffs him in shining silver restraints. Then, Roy climbs inside a wooden trunk and Siegfried pulls a cloth sack over his head. Siegfried ties up the sack and closes the lid of the trunk. He ties and locks it in seconds and climbs on top with one great stride. He pulls up a curtain and the audience is stunned when almost immediately Roy leaps to the stage in Siegfried's place. He unties the trunk as quickly as Siegfried tied it. He throws it open, unfastens the sack and impossibly, Siegfried is secured in his place. Holding his manacled arms aloft, Siegfried steps from the trunk and Roy frees him.

But Siegfried and Roy are just beginning. The best is yet to come. A great cage is wheeled onto the stage. Roy climbs inside, smiling and waving goodbye, as Siegfried locks the door. Seconds later a huge lion appears in Roy's place. Siegfried opens the cage and teases the snarling cat. It swings at him with its great paws. The audience, particularly people in the front rows, recoils instinctively.

Siegfried rolls the lion and its cage off-stage and returns to stage center carrying a beautiful black panther on his shoulders. "Would you like more?" he asks the audience. They shout enthusiastically. "They won't let me make a lion disappear," he says, "because it is the symbol of MGM. How about a 650-pound Bengal tiger instead?" The audience roars its approval.

This time the illusion is reversed. A huge tiger paces ominously in a cage. Siegfried covers the cage and it is hoisted high above the stage. He pulls

5. With a graceful leap, Siegfried jumps astride the trunk. In one continuous motion, he draws up a long curtain attached to a hoop. He lifts it up over his head...

6. ...and drops it to reveal the metamorphosis! The event takes no longer than it took for you to flick your eyes from one photograph to the next.

the cloth down and the tiger has vanished. Simultaneously, Roy appears in the cat's place below. Moments later the missing tiger materializes inside a trunk halfway down the stage. Exiting to the strains of *Born Free*, Siegfried and Roy wave majestically to the applauding audience.

Both Siegfried and Roy are originally from Germany. Siegfried has been involved with magic nearly all of his life. "I started out in the usual way," he says. "You know, one Christmas as a kid you get a magic set and then you buy a book. Later, I saw Kalanag perform in Munich. At fourteen I tried to put together a magic performance. It was a disaster. It was also a shock to the people in my town. They were used to seeing me in comedy, but I changed my image completely when I became a magician on stage. They couldn't picture it because they knew me as something else. They thought I was crazy to go into magic. But I didn't give up. I said, 'That is the way it's going to be.'"

On the other hand, Roy has always been involved with animals. His uncle was a zoo director, and he grew up surrounded by large cats. He had his own pet cheetah and dreamed of becoming a lion tamer. "When I used to talk about having many animals," he says, "everybody told me it couldn't happen. 'You've got a cheetah—be happy with that,' they said. But nothing could stop me."

Siegfried and Roy met in 1960, aboard the German cruise ship The Bremen. Both had decided to see the world. At that time in their lives, magic was a part-time occupation for Siegfried; animals a leisure-time passion for Roy. Roy was a steward and Siegfried a performer. "We met because I was performing on the ship," says Siegfried. "I did my little magic act—the rabbit out of the hat, swallowing razor blades, you know. Roy was watching every time. One day he came to me and said, 'Siegfried, if you can make a rabbit disappear, why don't you try it with a cheetah?' So I asked him where I could get a cheetah, and he told me he had a cheetah at home, but they wouldn't let him bring it on board the ship. At first I thought he was a little nutty. What kind of a story is that?"

"I asked him if he could make the cheetah vanish," says Roy, "just to find out what he would say. He thought I was joking because he hadn't ever met anybody who owned a cheetah. For the fun of it, he told me he could do it. So on the next cruise, I brought my cheetah on board and we were stuck with it. I hid it in my cabin. We decided to use it in the next performance. We were scared. We had a couple of drinks in the bar before the show. The people were crazy over the act, so we were given a permit to keep my cheetah on the ship."

During the five years they worked aboard German cruise ships, Siegfried and Roy learned the basics of performing magic with large animals. "The act," says Siegfried, "got bigger and bigger, and we had to make a decision about whether to continue as professional magicians or

7. Roy drops the curtain and takes a bow. But the metamorphosis is not yet complete.

not." They decided to stay in magic. After the cruise ships, the pair appeared on German television. Then they were invited to give a command performance for Princess Grace and Prince Rainier in Monte Carlo. "That was a big success," says Roy, "because the cheetah ran into the audience and the story made the front pages. After that came a contract for the Lido in Paris and then for Las Vegas."

"When other magicians can't believe we moved up so fast, they forget about the years aboard ship," says Siegfried. "For quite a while we had only the cheetah. But we realized that in order to be successful you have to be different. Roy got a tiger cub and raised him, then another, and then the lion. Now we have five big cats."

The men keep the cats with them at all times.

8. Jumping down from the trunk, Roy feverishly unties the ropes Siegfried tied before him.

9. Roy opens the trunk and unties the sack. Not only is Siegfried handcuffed inside, he is wearing a different costume!

They lounge in the yard of their home in Las Vegas. "The way we work with them depends on affection, on love, and contact," says Siegfried. "The animals must believe in us and trust us."

According to Roy, the lion roars every day at four o'clock. "The golfers on the course next door say it affects their shots," he says. "The neighbors are finally getting used to them. And we never have any burglars—especially with my sign BEWARE OF THE DOG."

In intensity and drama, Siegfried and Roy's act has the emotional impact of the large-scale extravaganzas produced by the old masters. But their approach is modern, resembling that of a superstar rock musician. "Why shouldn't there be a big show like Blackstone's?" asks Siegfried. "Of course, people are smarter today. But the interest is there. You have to use all the tools available, things like sound and light. You have to think like an audience and understand how it wants to be entertained."

In 15 years Siegfried has learned a lot about animals and I have learned a lot about magic," says Roy. "We are on top now but there is no limit to our minds. When you sit down and say this is it, you have already given up. When everything seems comfortable and easy, you become afraid that you might lose it. I am always thinking of tomorrow. We are young. Basically, we are gypsies."

"There's always something new," comments Siegfried. "When we were in the Lido, the first few months we thought, 'This is the top.' But that's not so. The next thing is also the top. The art is not getting in but staying in."

The effort Siegfried and Roy put into their act is apparent on stage, as is their joy in performing. They are exuberant entertainers. "We work because we love it," says Siegfried. "We are happy on stage and every performance is a challenge. Each one is different. The audience is different and the animals are different and we are different. I want to be liked. We need our audience."

"I love the animals," says Roy, "and I love magic. But entertaining is what I love most. We aren't interested in anything but live entertainment. To really see Siegfried and Roy, you have to come see us."

1. Siegfried rolls a great cage to the center of the stage. Snarling inside is Rajah, a four-year-old Siberian tiger who weighs 650 pounds.

2. The beautiful animal paces back and forth in the cage, following Siegfried's every movement. Siegfried drapes a cloth all around him.

3. When the cage has been completely covered, Siegfried brings up the four panels attached to the table below it, quickly fastening them at the corners.

4. Dangling from chains, the cage is lifted into the air. When it stops high above the stage, Siegfried whips the cloth aside. The tiger has vanished.

5. The instant the cloth falls to the stage revealing the disappearance of the tiger, Roy bursts into view on the table below.

6. A few seconds later, Siegfried walks down the stage to an unimportant-looking trunk. He opens it and out jumps the missing tiger. With Roy and Rajah majestically on top, Siegfried triumphantly leads the way. The spotlight follows the performers as the trunk is slowly drawn off the stage.

MENTALISM AND ESCAPES

Mentalism and escapes have the same objective as any other type of magic: to create the illusion of an impossible event. The mentalist reads another person's mind, correctly divines the location of hidden objects, or discloses the contents of a sealed envelope. The escape artist frees himself from ropes, chains, locks, handcuffs, straitjackets, and even jail cells. In either case, the performer on stage must focus the full attention of the audience on himself—on his seeming ability to defy natural laws.

Both mentalist and escapist must establish an atmosphere of credibility because the audience often cannot see for itself that the performer is really doing what he claims. To accomplish this, both presentations depend on verification from members of the audience and authorities of all sorts—local mayors, members of chambers of commerce, and police officials, for example. These outside participants inspect all props and certify that they have not been tampered with in any way and that the magician has not been allowed unsupervised access to them. In this way, the anticipated event is certified to be impossible.

Challenges become a heavily emphasized part of the performance. Mentalists refer to their effects as tests, and for some feats, outside individuals control the circumstances surrounding their execution. This is the situation when a mentalist is challenged to read the headline of a newspaper in a distant city before the editor prints it or to find something hidden by a committee of townspeople. Escape kings are similarly challenged to free themselves from bonds devised by onlookers. Handcuffs might be brought on the stage during a performance, or a group of individuals might offer a new device as a challenge to the artist.

Challenges from outside sources generally take the form of contract agreements. The challenger may establish test conditions. He may build or inspect equipment, subject to the performer's approval. Or the opposite takes place, with the performer devising details and the challenger approving them. In any event, testimonials from outsiders further ensure the performer's credibility—and have publicity value.

This style of performance—with all the attendant challenges—is very much a twentieth century phenomenon. Mind reading and divination, however, are hardly of recent origin. They can be traced back to the soothsayers and oracles, the seers and fortune-tellers of ancient times. Spiritualism had its beginnings in prehistory in the rites of ancestor worship. If the departed ancestors could see into human affairs, it was thought, then contact with them assured knowledge of future events. And this knowledge could be used to control the future. Methods of divination and fortune telling varied from culture to culture but have been practiced since antiquity.

Some believe that games of ancient origin—chess, cards, backgammon, and the like—evolved from the lot casting of early divinators. On a different level, the priestess at the Oracle of Apollo at Delphi delivered prophecies in what is assumed to have been a drugged state. One such sibyl asked Apollo to grant her as many years as there are grains in a handful of sand. The god complied, but she had not asked for physical immortality. Her body shriveled and disappeared. Her spirit remained in a cave and there she offered pronouncements in a disembodied voice. Sometimes she wrote predictions on leaves but she was careless and they blew away.

Gifts of prophecy have been associated with magicians through the centuries. The Magi, Merlin, Nostradamus, Cagliostro, and countless others foretold future events. On a more ordinary level, fortune-tellers read palms, faces and bumps on the head. In the Middle Ages they wandered the countryside, later evolving into the mediums and psychics so popular during the late nineteenth and early twentieth centuries.

The earliest type of mental routine performed on the classical stage was a two-person telepathy act called Second Sight. Robert-Houdin and his son, Émile, popularized this type of performance in Paris in the 1840s. In the early part of Houdin's career, before he had built any of his impressive large-scale illusions, this routine remained consistently more popular than either his straight magic or his automata. In the Second-Sight demonstration, Émile sat on the stage blindfolded. His father wandered through the audience collecting various articles. Émile then correctly identified whatever his father held up. Many of the astounded theater-goers became convinced that the boy possessed uncanny psychic abilities.

At about the same time that Robert-Houdin was enjoying success with his Second-Sight routine, an American Washington Irving Bishop was presenting similar mind-reading feats. Bishop employed an assistant who knew where various objects were hidden. Grasping the wrist of his ever-silent helper and questioning him aloud, Bishop was able to determine where the articles were secreted. (This technique is more correctly termed muscle reading than mind reading.)

Much of the spiritualism craze in America later in the nineteenth century can be traced to the Fox sisters who produced spirit manifestations in their farmhouse in New York state. Strange thumpings and tappings, with objects moving of their own accord, were attributed to the ladies' ability to contact the dead. Recognizing a good thing, the brothers Davenport, William Henry Harrison and Ira Erastus, from Buffalo, New York, borrowed the women's idea but took their act on stage. The brothers were bound hand and foot and put in their spirit cabinet. Strange sounds emanated from the structure. Bells rang and instruments played. But any time the cabinet was opened, the gentlemen were still securely bound. Spirits, they claimed, produced the clamor.

The Davenports had become famous enough to warrant a world tour. They were successful in London, but such noted conjurers as John Nevil Maskelyne and John Henry Anderson denounced them as frauds. These magicians duplicated the Davenports' demonstrations on stage, exposing their methods as simple deceptions—not psychic phenomena.

Anna Eva Fay, a famous stage psychic of the era, worked from the 1870s into the reign of vaudeville. She did a few magic tricks and had a spirit cabinet but was best known for her question-and-answer period when she made startling revelations. Later on, her daughter-in-law, Eva Fay, became well-known for similar feats. Vaudeville also worked well for a two-person second-sight routine. Bess and Harry Houdini performed such an act during the early days of their career. But it wasn't until the 1920s, when Joseph Dunninger came on the scene, that mentalism as it is performed today came into being. Dunninger was the first mentalist to perform alone on the stage. He simply sat in a chair, scribbling on a pad of paper, while he revealed the thoughts of members of his audience. His results were astounding and his showmanship superb. Dunninger never claimed to be a psychic, nor did he contact the spirit world, but some of his feats have never been duplicated.

Compared with mentalism, escapes are a recent specialization. It is likely that a primitive chieftain who wished to establish belief in his supernatural powers could impress his followers by proving himself able to escape from restraints. The fact that normal bonds could not hold him was not only proof of invulnerability but a symbolic escape from mortality itself. The magic of American Indians included several rope escapes.

Witches of the Middle Ages were thought to be capable of unbolting doors and slipping through keyholes in insubstantial form. But escapes do not have the glamorous history of mentalism. Street performers used them as attractions in a side-show atmosphere. They would tie up a man with a great hoopla. He would then refuse to release himself until the spectators had passed the hat.

Traditionally, many magicians have included escapes in their general repertoire. According to Houdini, a French magician named La Trude performed a handcuff release on stage as early as

1700. Later in the century, Pinetti escaped from locked chains, and John Henry Anderson nearly always included a few escapes in his show. Harry Houdini, however, was the first magician to become outstandingly successful as an escape artist. He is credited with raising the status of escapes to the level of a suspenseful stage performance. Until his time, they were merely stunts—an interlude between more spectacular acts.

Houdini was able to change public response to escapes by his incredible abilities as a showman. (There are those who consider Houdini the finest showman the world has ever seen, ranking him above the celebrated P. T. Barnum.) The potential for such a phenomenon, however, existed long before Houdini, and in his achievement lies the link between mentalism and escapes.

Escapes first gained public notoriety during Anderson and Maskelyne's campaign against the Davenports. (They were supposedly bound while in their cabinet.) Maskelyne went further than Anderson, however, and launched an attack on self-claimed psychics and spiritualists from the stage to the Egyptian Hall. When a London medium claimed to produce visible spirits during a seance, Maskelyne staged a similar demonstration. The ghostly form of a young woman appeared to emanate from his side. When another supposed psychic was reported able to float to the ceiling in the seance room, Maskelyne levitated himself to the top of the theater. There he leisurely stretched into a horizontal position, straightened, and returned to the stage.

This response of the magician—to take it upon himself to expose fraud—has ample precedent. Daniel similarly discredited the Babylonians to Cyrus of Persia, and early Christians delighted in explaining the illusions in pagan temples. In modern times, magicians have often become involved in controversy surrounding spiritualists because of personal experiences. During Bess and Harry Houdini's brief career as stage mediums, distraught members of the audience once requested Harry's aid. Friends in their community were being hoodwinked by a local medium, and they asked Houdini to help them prove the psychic fraudulent. Houdini duplicated the medium's effects. Much later Houdini became absorbed in a crusade against self-claimed psychics.

However, the magician's task is Herculean. He can only duplicate past occurrences of so-called psychic phenomena. He can do nothing to prevent the human tendency to believe. And he is doubly frustrated by the very nature of his art. On stage the magician, the mentalist or escape artist in particular, asks his audience to believe for a moment that he can actually perform miracles. If he is dramatically successful, some of his public may grant him the time-honored position of the magician-priest. Though both Dunninger and Houdini disclaimed any supernatural abilities and were zealous in their pursuit of fraud, both were credited with psychic powers.

In all types of magic, the magician strives to create the sensation of mystery. Much of the event being witnessed takes place in the mind of the spectator. The mind fills in blanks and creates a logical sequence of steps leading to the observed result, no matter how great a departure that result is from natural laws. With a close-up maneuver, a cabaret effect, or a large-scale illusion, a magician creates the image of a real event within the mind of the spectator. To use an exaggerated example, many people who went to see Harry Kellar expected to see on stage the little red devils that adorned his posters. "The people who came to the show expecting to see devils generally did see them, or thought they did," said Kellar, "all over the stage and even in the theater lobby, on the way out." He didn't have to perform a trick—his greatest prop was the imagination of his viewers.

Mentalists and escapists must also learn how to make the spectators' imagination work for them, but their magic is abstract. If coins seem to penetrate solid table tops, invisible birds are captured in butterfly nets, or women are casually truncated, the audience thinks it sees an impossible act taking place before its very eyes. When a mentalist or an escape artist performs, the audience doesn't have much to see. Some escapes, certain rope releases and handcuff escapes, are performed in view of the audience, but most are not. A curtain enclosed Houdini's Water Torture Cell and Milk Can. Similarly, escapes from packing crates were often performed underwater or otherwise out of sight. Of course, jailbreaks were not visible. Similarly, when a mentalist asks if a member of the audience is thinking of the initials L. M., and someone says, "Yes," there isn't much for the audience to look at. So the audience conjectures, and makes the connections in the same way it does when viewing an illusion show.

Left with a series of impressions from an entertaining performance of magic involving props, the dazzled audience asks, "How does he *do* it?" (The magician's stock answer is, "Very well.") The audience does not usually find explanations for the baffling things seen, but it knows the solutions are there in the props and the performer. When an audience sees a mentalist or an escapist, however, the situation is different. Possibly, what the viewers have seen has been verified by observers on the stage who are proxies for every member of the audience. But whether the viewers accept that the mentalist has received information using only his own perceptions or that the escape artist has freed himself from real restraints is primarily dependent upon the performer's dramatic abilities.

The dramatic values involved in mental routines and escapes are unique. A standard magician never tells his audience what he is going to do before he does it—for that would disturb the impact of the feat and reduce the mystery. A mentalist or an escape artist, however, must make a point of telling the audience what he is going to do next.

Blindfold drives or predictions of events of general interest are likely to be highly publicized. The more complicated and impossible these stunts seem and the greater the distances involved, the more impossible they appear. Anyone following such an event asks, "*Can* he do it?" But when a magician comes on stage to do standard magic effects, no one asks whether he is going to be able to perform the act or not. Without props, fancy lighting, or assistants, the mentalist creates suspense from the fact that most people cannot do what he is about to do. Sometimes his success gives rise to exaggerated accounts of his powers.

A similar situation occurs during an escape. Like all magicians, the escape artist possesses knowledge and skill that are not part of an ordinary person's experience. The escapist demonstrates this knowledge and skill by pitting himself against mechanical devices constructed for the express purpose of preventing his release. The escape artist subjects himself to the possibility of considerable discomfort, if not real harm.

The dramatic structure of a release is similar to that of a mentalism effect. Like the mentalist, the escapist elicits the question, "*Can* he do it?" The presence of locksmiths, police officials, or handcuff manufacturers to verify that the restraints have not been counterfeited increases the tension by increasing the odds against the magician. As the tension increases, the audience becomes more and more sympathetic. It begins to identify with the performer and to care about him. This emotional involvement is crucial to the performance but sometimes gives rise to an overestimation of the abilities of the person on stage.

A large number of people continue to attribute supernatural powers to performers. Public belief in such supposed powers becomes dangerous in the hands of an unscrupulous person. Despite attempts of magicians to debunk those who claim psychic ability, as E. M. Butler observed in *The Myth of the Magus*, "Lecky very truly said that where supernatural phenomena are concerned humanity believes in the teeth of the evidence, or disbelieves in spite of the evidence, but never because of the evidence."

Because of the intensity of the focus on the performer, the mentalist and the escape artist must assume roles a little different from other conjurers. Above all else, they must appear larger than life. Houdini and Dunninger were enormous personalities. Such enlargement helps a mentalist or an escapist to fill an empty stage. The type of magic he works requires a commanding presence, for there is nothing to take attention away from him—no pyrotechnics, no white birds fluttering, no pretty girls, not even the glitter of a silver coin. These are very demanding performances. The performer must confront his audience constantly. He must seduce its skeptical mind into believing that what it thought took place did take place. To catch the attention of the audience and hold it through a dramatic buildup to a climax, he needs an acute awareness of humanity as well as a full understanding of the nature of his art.

DUNNINGER

Master mentalist Joseph Dunninger astounded audiences on stage, television, and radio for nearly 50 years. Teams of mind readers had flourished throughout the nineteenth century and were good vaudeville attractions, but Dunninger was the first mentalist to work alone. He began with straight magic, tried escapes briefly, but found his mental exploits intrigued audiences the most. Dunninger first performed a magic routine in 1908 at the age of sixteen. Two years later he added some spiritualist effects. When he played in Hartford, Connecticut, in 1917, he presented a straitjacket escape. By 1919, he had become exclusively a mentalist. He performed at some public functions but usually worked at private parties. Until his radio show began in 1943, he was not widely known.

Dunninger has compared the development of his career with Harry Houdini's. Both were aware of the benefits of good publicity, and each was zealous in the pursuit of fraudulent mystics. Dunninger's style, however, was different. He affected flamboyant dress. He knotted dashing silk scarves around his throat and sported spats, fancy vests, and dramatic hats. Tall and broad shouldered, Dunninger wore his dark hair long, and he cultivated a hint of a British accent. Like Houdini, Dunninger accepted challenge tests from the audience and specialized in publicity stunts.

One of Dunninger's favorite publicity stunts was the Blindfold Drive. Blindfolded, he would drive an automobile to a destination he presumably knew only by mind reading. He describes the stunt's history in *Dunninger's Secrets: as Told to Walter Gibson:* "…Washington Irving Bishop… cooked up a publicity sensation known as the Blindfold Drive. A committee would hide an object anywhere in town; then they would blindfold Bishop, help him aboard a wagon, and join him there. He would take the reins, slap the horses, and they would go larruping down the street, around corners, on a mad chase that would wind up at the chosen destination, where Bishop would order the committee to help him to the sidewalk to continue the hunt…Rivals sprang up to compete with Bishop, and they all found that the hell-for-leather drive, with excited crowds dashing alongside, was

(Left) The Blindfold Drive was one of Dunninger's favorite publicity stunts. Accompanied by several public officials, Dunninger would drive blindfolded to a location unknown to him. There he would disembark and find a hidden object.

(Near right) Dunninger was the first mentalist to work alone on stage (mind-reading routines were previously done by duos). He was also the first to host a nationwide radio show.

(Far right) In the early days of his career, Dunninger performed jail escapes. The publicity surrounding a jailbreak was good, but not as good as that he received for his mental tests.

the only way to rouse the public to such a fever pitch that they would pack the local opera house to witness the mind-reading show that evening…All that went out with the horse and buggy, but the act itself was still good…So the newer version was for the mentalist to start from some advertised place like a hotel entrance or the theater lobby, where he was first blindfolded, then walk along between two committeemen." The blindfolded mentalist would lead the way to the hidden object. Dunninger found the automobile, when driven by a blindfolded man, to be quite as exciting as the horse and buggy.

Dunninger's challenges often took the form of mental projections—thought waves apparently sent over great distances. He might cite the headline of a newspaper yet to be printed in a distant city. Or he might reverse the procedure and claim to project a thought into an editor's mind hundreds of miles away. Like Houdini, the situation and test conditions were agreed upon by Dunninger and the challengers before the event.

Dunninger's usual performing style was to sit with a pad of paper and a pencil. He doodled while he called out names, initials, or numbers thought of by some member of his audience. When someone identified the information as his own, Dunninger would spell out names, identify the person's relationship to the questioner, read social security numbers, or serial numbers from bank notes. He would identify word for word a name and address, a sentence or a quotation written in a spectator's notebook. He often concluded a series of thought readings by asking, "Are you thinking of the word amazing? Is it in reference to me? Thank you very much." Dunninger offered $10,000 to anyone who could prove that he used stooges or confederates.

Dunninger would include tests in each show which later became known as brain busters. One of his most successful was the telephone-book test. "…I wrote a name on a sheet of cardboard that was placed in full view with its blank side toward the audience," he reported. "Then, a skeptical spectator was given an ordinary telephone book and told to open it at random. That done, he circled his hand over either page, finally stopping on a name and number which were verified by other persons. When the cardboard was turned around, it was found to bear that very name."

Dunninger never claimed supernatural or even supernormal powers in his thought reading. Also, he never claimed to be a mind reader. He referred to his ability as "telesthesia"—an impression received by a sense organ, but not a usual sense organ, and sometimes received from a distance. He described the process as follows: "You pick up a vivid impression from another mind and

141

The eyes and nose in Dunninger's mysterious symbol are drawn in the shape of a bat.

When Dunninger was a young man, most of his performances were given at private parties, and he was little known to the general public.

others follow or suggest themselves. But it isn't mind reading; it is thought reading. When a series of such thought impressions come in fairly close in succession, it takes on the semblance of mind reading, though if you check back, you may find that you have added links of your own making, just as you might piece together the fragments of a dream to form a waking continuity."

Besides telesthesia, Dunninger believed the mentalist uses "hyperesthesia," which is an intensification of the ordinary senses. A thought reader who concentrates deeply enough on his subject might pick up an unconscious but audible whisper not heard by the ordinary person. Dunninger asserts that such phenomena are perfectly within the realm of everyday life. "Take the proofreader who can spot misspelled words by simply glancing at a printed page...the nonsmoker who can smell a cigarette before someone lights it."

The third tool of the master mentalist was always a thorough knowledge of his art. Describing the necessary technique for a successful enactment of a blindfold drive, Dunninger notes, "Any competent performer should know how to size up a committee and handle them accordingly. Otherwise he shouldn't be posing as a mentalist." Skeptics might argue over Dunninger's ability to perceive thought waves, but his ability to perceive human reactions was undeniable. He operated on the assumption that people have a tendency to believe almost anything if they are so inclined. He was careful in the selection of participants in his tests and he employed a sort of mental misdirection. Dunninger suggested constraints on tests that seemed to prevent deception, but actually allowed for it. He explained why one impromptu test worked so well: "I stressed as absolute precautions the very factors that were making the result possible."

Dunninger considered mentalists halfway between magicians and mediums. "Some (mentalists) rely greatly on magical methods while others attempt actual tests in ESP," he said. "However far the pendulum swings, a capable mentalist will come through with results that a dyed-in-the-wool magician could never touch because a mentalist plays hunches and realizes how often they may come through." And a mentalist doesn't have to advertise perfect results. Dunninger himself only claimed 90 percent accuracy.

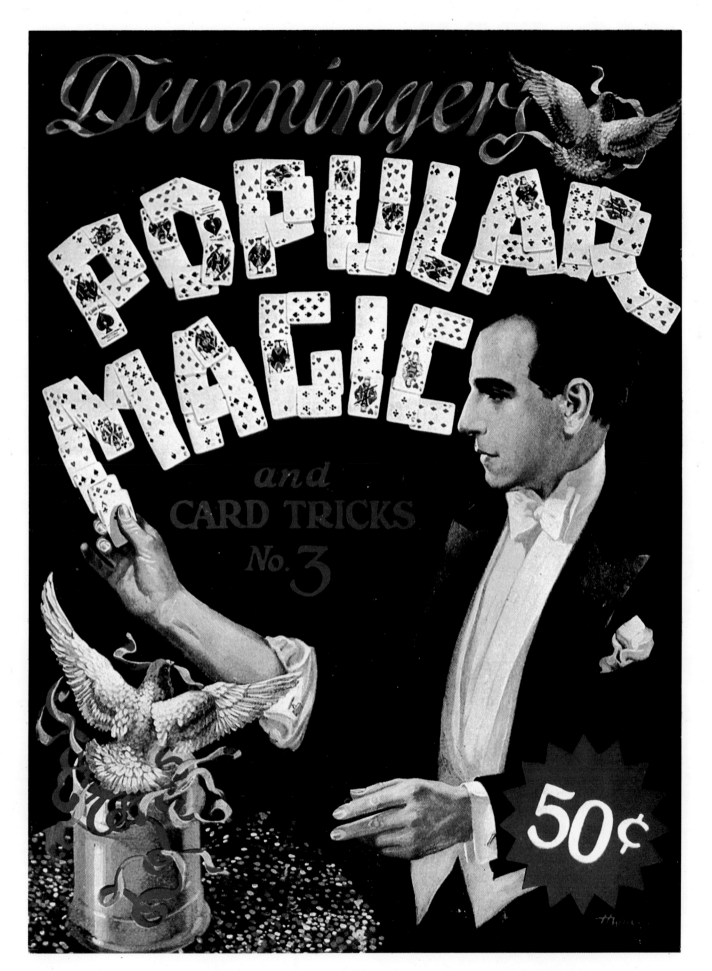

HOUDINI

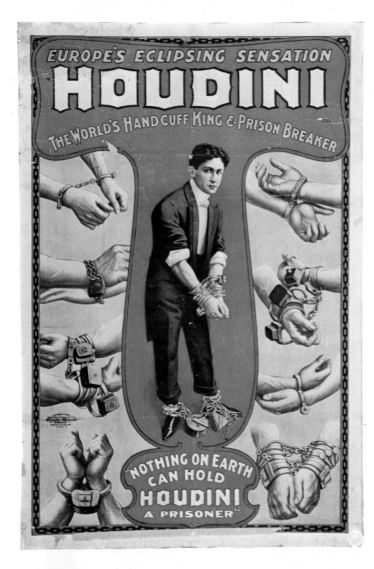

figure of world renown. In *Houdini: His Life-Story by Harold Kellock from the documents and recollections of Beatrice Houdini*, his career is described as "the dream of an inspired press agent," who, more often than not, was Houdini himself. He was emotional, egotistical, forceful and intense, a dynamo of hard work and dedication.

Some might view Houdini as a daredevil with a low-life occupation, a performer of side-show stunts who achieved fame by a fluke. Before Houdini performed them, escapes had little theatrical stature. It is part of his peculiar genius that he developed such feats into suspenseful theater productions. He certainly never minimized the potential danger or physical discomfort of his stunts, but his appeal cannot be attributed merely to sensationalism. He stressed the many precautions he had taken to insure his safety. Devices were constructed to guard against accidents, and well-trained assistants were always near at hand.

Occasionally, Houdini underestimated the difficulty of a stunt and endangered himself. The majority of his feats, however, were strenuous but not dangerous to a man in good physical condition. More important than the physical danger of Houdini's stunts was their apparent impossibility.

Houdini was a master publicist. His ability to keep his name in the newspapers was quite as impressive as his prowess at escapes. Here, he is trussed up in tires and snow chains.

The life story of Harry Houdini is the material from which legends are made. In fact, with a sure instinct for publicity, he fabricated many of these legends himself. His personality was enigmatic — a collage of tyrannical rages, impetuous generosities, compelling bravado, puritanism, shyness, hypersensitivity, an all-encompassing family loyalty and devotion to work. Freudians could have a heyday analyzing Houdini's worship of his mother, his fascination with insane asylums and graveyards, even his occupation. Devotees of the philosophy of the self-made man have a perfect case history in the rise of Ehrich Weiss, the son of an impoverished immigrant rabbi from Hungary who became Houdini, a

He created situations from which it seemed no living human could escape—then he did so with just the right amount of trouble. Although he took great pains to disclaim supernatural abilities, there were those who refused to believe him. Some people insisted that Houdini could dematerialize himself and slip through keyholes like the wizards of old.

Houdini described his genius as the mastery of fear and the ability to keep calm under any circumstance. He combined these skills with an unremitting attention to detail in the construction and presentation of his illusions. It took him years to develop the dramatics that would make the escapes work on stage as entertainment. He had to learn how to build suspense properly: there is little drama in an escape done too quickly, for the audience thinks it is easy and ceases to care. But if an escape takes too long, particularly if it is performed out of sight, the audience becomes restless.

Houdini discovered that some releases, like his Straitjacket Escape, had more dramatic impact if they were performed in full view of the audience. Others, such as his Milk Can Escape and Chinese Water Torture Cell, could not be performed in full view without exposing the secret. In the first,

Houdini was padlocked in a large steel milk can filled with water. In the second, he was lowered head first, with his feet manacled, into a mahogany-and-glass cabinet filled with water. Underwater escapes like these were not too lengthy—a few minutes at most. Houdini challenged members of the audience to hold their breath while he worked behind a curtain.

Houdini also learned that some releases were not worth the effort. For example, his escape from a wetsheet was much more taxing than the audience assumed. (A wetsheet was intended to calm and restrain a disturbed patient; he was wrapped tightly in sheets saturated with warm water.) It took Houdini half an hour of strenuous exertion to free himself. Although he performed the escape in full view, the audience was unable to identify with the situation inside the clinging muslin.

This process of identification was crucial to Houdini's performance. Often time-consuming releases had to be accomplished behind a curtain. It seems impossible that anyone could hold an audience spellbound for half an hour while hidden from view. Houdini convinced people that his struggle against the odds was also their own. They strained with him and shared his triumph. It was his boyish

and open smile, they say, that won the hearts of every audience after each escape left him standing free of some outlandish restraint.

Houdini's choice of magic as a career may seem perplexing. His intelligence and mechanical skill were formidable and his energy awesome. Like any other performer, Houdini concentrated on his strongest skills, and his career, like any other, evolved through the years. He began as a conventional magician, and he always presented some standard magic as well as escapes. One of his standbys was his famous Needle Trick. Houdini would swallow several packets of needles and a length of thread. Then, he would produce a string of threaded needles from his mouth. His Vanishing Elephant, not performed until his last tour, is quite as much a part of Houdini-lore as his escapes. He even performed impromptu sleight of hand from time to time. But Houdini became a household name as an escape artist, and these exploits were known around the world.

Harry Houdini (opposite) married Bess Rahner (left) after a two-week courtship. At first, her mother was violently opposed to the match, but Cecilia Weiss, Houdini's mother, welcomed the young couple into her home.

(Below and opposite) Challenge tests were generally worked out in advance, with both parties agreeing to certain conditions.

(Below) The Metamorphosis was the climax of Bess and Harry Houdini's early show.

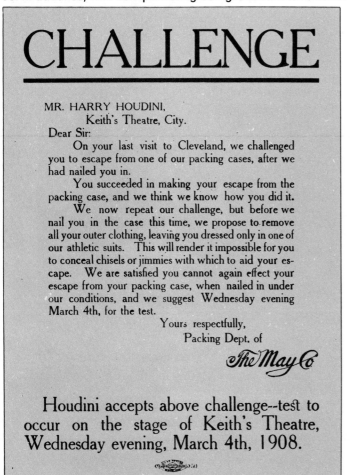

CHALLENGE

MR. HARRY HOUDINI,
    Keith's Theatre, City.
Dear Sir:
    On your last visit to Cleveland, we challenged you to escape from one of our packing cases, after we had nailed you in.
    You succeeded in making your escape from the packing case, and we think we know how you did it.
    We now repeat our challenge, but before we nail you in the case this time, we propose to remove all your outer clothing, leaving you dressed only in one of our athletic suits. This will render it impossible for you to conceal chisels or jimmies with which to aid your escape. We are satisfied you cannot again effect your escape from your packing case, when nailed in under our conditions, and we suggest Wednesday evening March 4th, for the test.
        Yours respectfully,
        Packing Dept. of
            The May Co

Houdini accepts above challenge--test to occur on the stage of Keith's Theatre, Wednesday evening, March 4th, 1908.

The Weiss family, which eventually included seven sons and one daughter, left Budapest for Appleton, Wisconsin, in 1874. The family moved to New York 14 years later. As a rabbi, Samuel Weiss found it difficult to make ends meet. When he died in 1892, the support of his wife was left to his sons. Houdini swore he would take care of his mother and he did—in his own inimitable fashion. He once showered his mother with $1000 in gold coins (a week's salary). In Europe, he bought her a dress that had been made for Queen Victoria and staged a party for her during which she sat on a throne.

Cecilia Weiss maintained that her son, Ehrich, who grew up to become Houdini, never cried as an infant. Like most boys, he found magicians fascinating. But it was not until he was sixteen that he discovered the *Memoirs of Robert-Houdin.* With Jack Hayman, a friend from the necktie factory where he worked, Ehrich devised a magic show and billed himself *Eric the Great.* Hayman told Ehrich that adding an "i" to a word meant "like" in French. Ehrich then adopted the name of Houdini, intending to be known as "like Houdin."

EX-POLICE CONSTABLES' CHALLENGE

HOUDINI,   Bedford Music Hall, Camden Town, N.W. 1.

Dear Sir,—We, the undersigned Committee, having served more than ONE HUNDRED YEARS between us in the METROPOLITAN POLICE DEPARTMENT, would like to know if we could challenge you to escape out of an

OBSOLETE PADDED CELL SUIT

This restraint holds the prisoner from the neck down to and including the feet; is made from extra heavy canvas and bound with leather. Your arms to be crossed in front and buckled behind your back. In addition, four belting straps encircling your body, so as to make you utterly helpless.

The only condition under which we will put you to the test, is that if you accept the challenge, you must RELEASE YOURSELF IN FULL VIEW OF THE AUDIENCE, to prove you obtain no secret assistance.

(Signed),

ex-P.C. TOM CROWTHER, 12, Winslow Rd., Fulham Palace Rd., Hammersmith, W.6 (30 yrs.' service)
P.C. WILLIAM GRAINGER, 19, Sancroft Street, Kennington Cross (27½ years' service).
P.C. ALBERT DEAN, 10, Priory Road, South Lambeth (27½ years' service).
P.C. ALFRED DAVEY, 35, Ambergate Street, Kennington (27 years' service).

Houdini accepts challenge—second performance, Friday night, May 21st, 1920, at the Bedford Music Hall, Camden Town, N.W. 1, under the condition that all straps encircling his neck MUST NOT BE DRAWN SO TIGHTLY AS TO CAUSE STRANGULATION.

John Waddington Ltd., Printers, 108, Albion Road, Stoke Newington, N. 16., and at Leeds.

Soon Harry Houdini quit the necktie factory to become a professional magician. He learned rope ties and handcuff escapes as he worked at Huber's Museum on 14th Street in New York. With the help of his young brother Theo, Houdini put together his own version of the Metamorphosis. The pair worked at the Chicago World's Fair of 1893 and at Chicago's Kohl and Middleton's Dime Museum. Back in New York in 1894, Houdini met and married Bess Rahner while he was working at Coney Island. According to Milbourne Christopher in *Houdini: The Untold Story*, Bess was a member of a song-and-dance team called the Floral Sisters. Soon Bess replaced Theo in the Metamorphosis.

Billed as *The Houdinis*, Bess sang and danced, Harry did handcuff escapes and sleight-of-hand tricks, and both performed the Metamorphosis. They worked in dime museums and beer halls of small towns in the Midwest and South. They were elated when they were finally booked by Tony Pastor in New York, but after the engagement they found themselves traveling with the Welsh Brothers Circus and the American Gaiety Girls. Then they traveled to Nova Scotia with Marco the Magician. The run was an economic disaster. But Houdini visited an insane asylum and was inspired to try a straitjacket escape on stage.

Just before the turn of the century, Houdini devised a scheme of challenging constables to try to restrain him in the towns where he played. The stunt was good publicity, and Houdini would secure a testimonial from the officers in order to help him enlist the support of the next police chief. In 1899, he talked his way into a Chicago jail. His successful escape was reported in the newspapers and attracted the attention of Martin Beck, an agent for the Orpheum circuit. Beck sent Houdini on tour on the condition that he would drop standard magic and concentrate on escapes, particularly on challenge escapes. Beck later recalled that he found Harry Houdini quite shy.

At the time Europe welcomed vaudeville acts. Unable to obtain further bookings in New York, Houdini left for London in 1900. He won a job at the Alhambra Theatre by successfully escaping from the formidable irons of Scotland Yard. In London, Houdini discovered that his handcuff escapes were more dramatic if he kept his head in view, although his hands and feet were hidden by a curtain. This increased the authenticity of the feat; Houdini could advertise that he performed "in full view" without exposing his techniques.

Houdini also continued the challenges which were to keep his name in the public mind throughout his long career. He would brazenly ask anyone in the audience with a pair of cuffs that might restrain him to bring them on stage. But stage challenges were fraught with problems. It was not always possible to control the situation. Once Houdini was locked into cuffs that had been tampered with so that they were impossible to open. Another time he was bound so tightly that his arms turned blue. Eventually, he learned how to deal with an unlikely challenge: he would promise to ac-

nailed inside and again after his escape. In Hanover, he first presented a straitjacket escape but performed it inside a cabinet. It fell flat but not the next time when he writhed on stage. In one year, Houdini had moved from being an unknown dime-museum entertainer to becoming a headliner in European vaudeville. By 1905, his fame had crossed the Atlantic, and he was booked in New York.

Bridge leaps, packing-crate escapes, and jailbreaks continued to be standard ways for Houdini to gain publicity. He escaped from the cell that had held the assassin of President Garfield, and on a cold day in November 1906, he jumped off the Belle Isle Bridge in Detroit. Houdini's description of the incident gave rise to one of his most widely circulated legends. In Houdini's version, the jump took place in December, and the Detroit River was frozen solid except for a hole big enough to accommodate Houdini. It was reported that he practiced for the stunt in a bathtub full of ice.

When interest in his exploits slackened around 1908, Houdini introduced the Milk-Can Escape. It became the spectacular climax to his show and revived public enthusiasm. Later the same year, Houdini returned to Europe. He no longer

When Sir Arthur Conan Doyle endorsed spirit photographs taken by Alexander Martin as genuine, Houdini made his own.

cept the offer at a later date. This solution had the double advantage of allowing Houdini to formulate a plan while ensuring some percentage of repeat attendance. In time Houdini did away with stage challenges in favor of escapes from devices supplied by corporations, government agencies, and individuals. He freed himself from a giant football, an enormous paper bag (without tearing the paper), a preserved giant squid, a mail pouch, an iron boiler, and other contraptions.

After completing a successful run in London, Houdini toured the continent. Manacled in irons in Dresden, he dove from a bridge and escaped underwater for the first time. The press coverage was extravagant. Also in Germany, he developed his first packing-crate escape. The crates were displayed for public inspection before Houdini was

featured handcuffs nor did he invite challengers on stage. Countless imitators had overworked handcuffs, and stage challenges were no longer feasible.

While Houdini was in Europe, his mother died. For months he was paralyzed with grief. By 1914, he had recovered sufficiently to present an illusion show in Edinburgh which featured no escapes. More successful was the Water Torture Cell, first presented in Germany later that year.

In the United States in 1918, at the suggestion of his brother Theo, Houdini performed the Straitjacket Escape suspended upside down above the crowd. By this time Theo was also famous as Hardeen, magician and escape artist. The following year Houdini discovered film; he appeared in three serials and two feature-length movies. According to William Lindsay Gresham, author of

The Man Who Walked Through Walls, the serials were "no worse than most." The first of the full-length features, *The Grim Game*, was the most successful. But many viewers credited trick photography with the escapes—not Houdini.

In 1922, while making a personal appearance tour to promote his films, Houdini began to speak out against fraudulent spiritualists. He enlivened

his lectures with demonstrations of the medium's art. Houdini packed houses with the same success as when he had performed escapes. The following year he joined a committee organized by the *Scientific American* magazine to investigate mediums. A $2,500 reward was offered to any person who could demonstrate actual psychic phenomena. When Boston medium Mina Crandon, who called herself Margary, claimed the money, Houdini was called in as a consultant. He discredited Margary by duplicating her results. In 1924, Houdini published *A Magician Among the Spirits*. It was acclaimed by those who shared his skepticism; criticized by those who did not.

Houdini's work with the *Scientific American* committee was responsible for one of his most spectacular feats. In 1926, Egyptian mystic Rahman Bey claimed he could control his bodily functions by psychic ability. As a demonstration, Bey put himself into a trance and remained in a sealed box under water for an hour. At the age of 52, Houdini duplicated the feat except he stayed under water for an hour and a half. The secret, he told reporters, was simply to remain calm and breathe regularly.

In September of 1925, Houdini toured with his last full-evening show. It featured two and a half hours of magic, and Houdini was on stage nearly all the time. In his own words it was all "Houdini stuff." He performed magic tricks, escapes, and then exposed spiritualist effects. For the first time in years, Bess joined her husband on stage in performing the Metamorphosis.

In Montreal in 1926, Houdini was speaking with three McGill University students backstage. One of them, J. Gordon Whitehead, asked Houdini if it was true that he could be punched without sustaining injury. Houdini said it was true. The student immediately landed four blows in the master magician's abdomen.

After the show closed that night, Harry and Bess traveled from Montreal to Detroit. Characteristically, Houdini refused to admit that he was in pain. That evening he went on stage as planned. After the show, he finally weakened and allowed himself to be taken to a hospital. He died a week later, on Hallowe'en, October 31, 1926, after two operations, the first to remove a ruptured appendix, the second to try to relieve peritonitis.

(Right) Houdini headlined this variety show bill. The Water Torture Cell, his own invention, was one of his most exciting escapes.

(Above and opposite) Houdini performed all manner of daring escapes in his first feature film. He escaped from a jail cell, released himself from a straitjacket while hanging upside down from the top of a building, and effected a plane-to-plane transfer in midair.

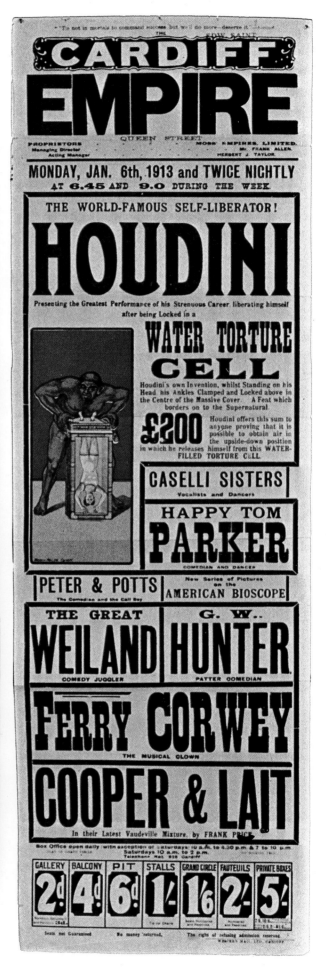

"It's all in the mind," says mentalist Maurice Fogel as he introduces his routine. His act is composed of different thought-reading tests and a spectacular divination.

MAURICE FOGEL

aurice Fogel performs several mental feats at the beginning of his routine. He asks the audience to think of colors or locations which he guesses correctly, or he guesses the amount of money in a man's pocket to the penny. But all this is overshadowed by his version of the one truly dangerous feat in magic—the Bullet Catch. Fogel calls his presentation Russian Roulette.

For this act, Fogel invites on stage a member of the audience who feels qualified to handle firearms. He asks the man to select at random one of six loaded air rifles in a revolving rack. Next he asks the man to fire the rifle at one of six glass plates suspended on a wooden frame, breaking it. The discharged rifle is returned to the rack. As the rack is revolved, the rifle is lost among the others. Fogel then invites five more similarly qualified spectators to join him on stage. He asks each of the six men to select a rifle and pick a number from one to nine.

Now Fogel goes to the frame of the targets and removes a sealed envelope which has been there throughout the performance. It contains a number written before the performance began.

One of the men opens the envelope and reads the number. The man who chose the number in the envelope steps aside; the other five are asked to aim their rifles at the five remaining targets. The sixth, the man with the predicted number, is told to aim at Fogel's forehead. Surprisingly, the sixth man rarely refuses to fire.

On a few occasions, Fogel has missed in his prediction. The pellet in an air rifle is not capable of killing a man but it can put out an eye. "Well, it was awkward. Part of the audience thought it was showmanship and a bit of catsup," he says. "I've done this show for magicians and they congratulate me on the showmanship. The fact is that it's not entirely showmanship—I'm genuinely nervous until it's over. Sometimes a fellow will miss a plate. It's frightening because I don't know where that bullet has gone. But I think it's a good number. I love doing it. I sort of get a reaction late, you know. It sets in when I start thinking about it."

The Bullet Catch intrigued Fogel as a child. "I come from a very, very poor family. We lived in a ghetto in the slums of London. My weekly pocket money was about threepence—that's equivalent to five cents or a dime—so consequently I couldn't

1. Fogel asks a member of the audience to concentrate on a location while he simultaneously writes it on a slate.

2. Fogel asks the participant to announce his choice and to reveal Fogel's writing. They are the same.

1. During his Russian Roulette, Fogel calls for a member of the audience, familiar with rifles, to assist him. On stage is a revolving rack containing six identical air rifles, each loaded with a single charge. He asks the person to select a rifle and to fire at any one of six china plates. The person then returns the discharged rifle to the rack which is spun, like the barrel of a revolver, so that the discharged rifle is now unidentifiable. Fogel then calls for five additional volunteers.

2. All six volunteers then select a rifle and each is asked to choose a number between one and ten. Fogel's earlier number prediction is in the envelope with a question mark.

socialize much with the lads. My favorite form of recreation was reading in public libraries which had the advantage of being free.

"I came across a magic book when I was about eleven or twelve years old and got the magic bug. In the classroom I showed one or two tricks and I felt a bit superior. I could do something the other fellow couldn't do. In one particular book I discovered that Houdini said that he was too nervous to present the bullet-catching feat. It became my ambition to present it.

"I had my first chance to study a rifle when I went into the army in 1940. During basic training I devised two or three methods by which the Bullet Catch could be presented. One time they were running a charity show, and I went to the entertainment officer with an idea to pull in the crowds: catching a live bullet between my teeth. Well, he

3. The man who has chosen the number in the envelope is instructed to aim his rifle directly at Fogel's forehead. The other five are to fire at the remaining plates.

thought I was crackers. I guess if someone approached me with the feat and I had never heard of it, I would think he was crackers too. But I eventually made a feature of it with the troops."

Fogel came to the fore as an entertainer during his army days, performing for British troops around the world. He continued to present the Bullet Catch but also developed a mentalist routine. "I went into mentalism," he says, "in order to evolve an act that didn't need props because of the constraints of the war. I found that it was a good attraction on the bill, and I was happy doing it. I think mentalism is the most adult form of magic."

Fogel presented the Bullet Catch commercially in theaters after the war but was forced to discontinue the stunt. "I needed a firearms certificate from Scotland Yard," he explains, "and they became difficult. So for some years I just per-formed my mentalism routine. Then I had the notion of the Russian Roulette with air rifles. The plot is good and there is an element of danger. I think it's really much more magical than the Bullet Catch because there's a gamble in it.

"I want to stress my supreme confidence in assessing calculated risk. It is something that I believe in strongly. All of us have a conscious and an unconscious, but I don't think we take sufficient advantage of the unconscious. I don't believe in fortune telling and I have yet to make up my mind whether there is such a thing as destiny. I don't think so. I don't pretend to be supernormal, but I do claim that each one of us has a divine spark. We should try to learn...try to realize how wonderful each one of us is. We each possess the most wonderful computer: our brain, our mind, and our soul which cannot be defined."

4. As five rifle-shots sound, shattered porcelain from five plates flies in every direction. The sixth rifle, aimed at Fogel, is harmlessly empty. Once again Fogel's prediction has proven correct. Nonetheless, he cannot restrain himself from flinching. Small wonder—three times his divination was wrong and he was injured on stage.

Announcing a slate test he has never before performed on stage, mentalist Glenn Falkenstein resorts to a traditional good luck gesture; he crosses his fingers.

GLENN FALKENSTEIN

Glenn Falkenstein's father owned a nightclub in Chicago, and as a boy, Falkenstein was fascinated by the magicians who performed there, especially by the sleight-of-hand effects they practiced to amuse one another before going on stage. At fifteen, Falkenstein got a job demonstrating magic at Abbott's Magic Store. "One day Harlan Tarbell came into the store," Falkenstein remembers. "I knew then I wanted to do a blindfolded mental act someday." (Harlan Tarbell wrote a major home-study course in magic in the 1920s and presented an impressive blindfold act.)

Falkenstein performed magic in high school and college. When he was in the Air Force during the Korean War, he won several contests with his routine. After his discharge from the Air Force, Falkenstein returned to school and earned a bachelor's degree in education. He moved to California in 1965 to continue school. He found a Saturday job at the Hollywood Wax Museum, frightening people. "It was fun at first," he says, "but after a couple of months it began to bore me; so I started doing magic shows instead. I used a little mentalism in the act. I was fascinated with the way people received my mental work. By the time the year was out, I was doing a whole mental act. Then I decided to do two acts, one magic and one mental. That's when I developed the act I'm doing now. I would do the magic act first, and people would stay to see the mental act. In 1968, Milt Larsen hired me to work weekends at The Magic Castle. Then I was a guest star on several radio programs and eventually was given my own show."

Falkenstein's mental routine on stage is short but fast paced and exciting. As he begins the act, he invites several people on stage to blindfold him. He has them inspect two half-dollars which he places over his eyes. They are secured in place with eight pieces of two-inch adhesive tape. Then, the mentalist dons a steel mask which is also inspected by the audience committee. Finally he invites a group of people on stage who hold various bills and identification cards. Groping, stumbling, and reaching blindly, Falkenstein correctly divines what is written on them.

Removing his blindfold, Falkenstein's grand finale is a slate test. Four members of the audience each choose a number from 100 to 1000. As they select their numbers, Falkenstein writes the amount these numbers will total on a slate. When the participants reveal their numbers, Falkenstein totals them on a second slate. The figures agree.

"There's a fine line between the occult and mentalism," says Falkenstein. "If people see a magician do a miracle, they say to themselves, 'It's a miracle, but there's a trick somewhere.' But with a mentalist there are no props. You say right off that it's a trick, but people tend not to believe you. People thought Houdini had special gifts, but he claimed only to be a magician.

"I think anyone who claims himself to be a psychic is limiting himself to a certain fringe of the population and because of that limitation I think he's hurting himself. I can look back on some very famous psychics who were around for a year or two and forgotten."

1. Falkenstein puts two half-dollars over his eyes and holds them in place with strips of adhesive tape.

2. Members of the audience verify that the half-dollars cover Falkenstein's eyes and that the tape is secure.

3. When fully blindfolded, Falkenstein covers the layers of tape and the coins underneath with a steel mask.

KRESKIN

Kreskin calls his two-and-a-half-hour programs *concerts* and the term is apt. The structure of his performance is episodic. Each segment builds to a crescendo of mystery mixed with hilarity. The string of demonstrations reinforces the credibility of his apparent thought reading. Whatever the audience may feel at the beginning, it goes away puzzling over what it has seen.

Kreskin begins by dashing rapidly through the theater, distributing slips of paper. He asks the recipients to write any questions or thoughts they would like him to receive. When he returns to the stage, he begins a monologue to introduce himself. His voice is warm and his speech well paced. "I do not perform miracles," he says. "It's a mystery." His style is anecdotal. For example, he talks about the time an airline lost his luggage. "If you're such a mentalist," snapped a harassed clerk, "why don't you know where your luggage is?"

In the first half of the program Kreskin performs a series of mental tests. They move from standard magic-oriented feats into the realm of thought reading. He may invite three spectators to join him on stage and borrow a ring from each. He then links and unlinks their rings. Each spectator verifies that his ring is indeed linked to the other two. Next, Kreskin may perform a Card Clairvoy-

ance effect. He invites two more people to join him on stage. He shuffles a deck of cards and asks each participant to draw out a section of 12 or 15 cards. He lists correctly the cards each spectator holds.

After these preliminary demonstrations, Kreskin moves on to thought reading. "I get a color," he says. "Orange, I think. The thought comes in clearly. Is there someone here who is thinking of burnt orange?" A woman seated in the theater titters and admits she is thinking of the color of her nail polish. Next, he might read her social security number. He may reproduce a drawing done by a member of the audience or describe a garment someone is thinking of buying.

At the end of the first half of the show, Kreskin performs his most spectacular feat. Every time he presents a concert, he asks a committee to hide his check somewhere in the theater. He leaves the theater under guard. When he returns, he asks a member of the committee to concentrate on where the check is hidden. He stresses that there is to be no verbal communication. If Kreskin cannot find his check, he forfeits his fee for the evening. He offers $20,000 to anyone who can prove he uses confederates or accomplices.

"There's no one else in the world doing this test regularly," says Kreskin. "I spent five years developing it." The committee can be creative in devising hiding places. During a show at Northwestern University, Kreskin's fee was found under a man's upper plate while he was wearing it. At the Waldorf Astoria in New York, it was in the

1. Kreskin leaves the theater while his check is hidden. He asks one young woman to help him find it.

2. He cautions her not to speak but asks her to hold one end of his handkerchief. Apparently, this is all the help he needs.

1. Kreskin links together three finger rings contributed by members of the audience.

2. After he has successfully linked the rings, Kreskin spins them around the end of a pencil.

Sometimes Kreskin does an advance test. Long before the program he asks someone involved in the production of his show, perhaps the master of ceremonies, to write down a thought. Then Kreskin reveals what it is during the performance.

stuffing of a turkey. "I kept getting the word turkey," he says. "At first I thought it was a comment on the performance. In all honesty it's a test which I do not enjoy doing. It has given me great press coverage, but I have failed a few times. Once it happened in New Zealand. Believe me, it was not a happy feeling to fly to New Zealand and do a free two-and-a-half-hour show."

The second half of Kreskin's program is a demonstration of what he calls "suggestology." Some years ago he would have termed this section a demonstration of hypnosis. "I have come to the conclusion that the hypnotic trance and the hypnotic state that the American Medical Association and the American Psychological Association have accepted do not exist," he says. "The turning point of my life came in my twenties when I found that I didn't have to hypnotize anybody to have them do some very dramatic things. People have been doing the wildest things for years on game shows without being hypnotized. They are paid or they are inspired by a good quiz master. I am not a hypnotist because to be considered a hypnotist would imply that I place people in altered states of consciousness. I don't."

Kreskin maintains that he only manipulates the attention of his audience. "Lend me your imagination," he asks. He begins by bringing as many people on stage as will comfortably fit. After he watches them through a series of small stunts, he sends about half back to their seats. He keeps 20 or 30 people on stage. They subsequently perform a series of antics. Kreskin grasps the hand of one young woman and shakes it violently. "Now, we forget things in everyday life, don't we?" he inquires. The girl nods. "What's your name?" he asks. She is completely at a loss. She stands for the rest of the program unable to remember her name.

A young man becomes convinced that it is warm in the theater. He removes his jacket at Kreskin's suggestion and wipes his forehead with his handkerchief. Two other men also remove their coats and following Kreskin's instructions, put them on inside out. At the end of the program, also

A bevy of audience participants wildly shake their arms at Kreskin's suggestion. He can persuade people on stage to do almost anything.

at Kreskin's suggestion, each will laugh at the other for having his coat on backwards. Neither remembers that his own coat is also on backwards.

Kreskin tells one woman that she will experience a sharp pinch whenever she hears a certain noise and that she will blame the man sitting behind her. At Kreskin's indication, she jumps to her feet and glares malevolently at the person behind her. Kreskin laughs and describes the situation on stage as an organized riot.

"A magician," says Kreskin, "captures the imagination of the audience and makes it suspend judgment as he explains the phenomena taking place. In the traditional sense I don't consider myself a magician, and I think I can separate my work from that of other mentalists as well. I have combined the principles of suggestion—the principles that in some way were the background of the traditional mentalist—with the drama of a magician's effects. I take the basic plot of revealing someone's thoughts or projecting an idea into someone's mind and dramatize it, using the license of the traditional magician."

Kreskin presents himself as humorous and affable, a calming and enjoyable person. His viewers relax and go along with him. By the end of the evening, most people find their credulity substantially stretched. "When Thurston performed his levitation, he created the impression that he held a woman in the air with his mind," says Kreskin. "His spectators were convinced that if they disturbed him in any way she would fall. The same kind of thing took place during Houdini's escapes. Most of what was happening was unseen. Perhaps the greatest mystery is in the unseen: the imagination is much more capable of producing mystery than anything that can be seen."

Kreskin was inspired by a fictional wizard, Mandrake the Magician. "I guess I was about five years old when I was given a comic book about the magician who gestured hypnotically and changed guns into flowers," he recalls. "I think it was good that my early perspective was not from the framework of the magic trick. Mandrake somehow used his mind. It became my ambition to do things that seemed to involve people's perceptions without using any machinery or other gimmicks.

By the time I was eight years old, the public library in Caldwell, New Jersey, gave me permission to read their adult psychology section. I had consumed it, though not in any great depth, by the time I was eleven or twelve and I knew there was more to psychology than gesturing hypnotically or believing in extrasensory perception."

"A second influence on my career came in the fourth grade when I played the children's game called Hot and Cold. The person who is 'it' must find something hidden by his classmates, following their verbal cues of 'hot' for getting closer or 'cold' for being off the trail. I thought perhaps it would be possible to find something without any verbal cues at all. I used to practice finding pennies I coerced my little brother into hiding for me.

The third influence on my career was a negative one—Adolf Hitler. His seeming power frightened me, and I began to study extensively the phenomena of so-called mass hypnosis."

Kreskin obtained a degree in psychology from Seaton Hall University in New Jersey. He has thought a great deal about his work and what he believes about the phenomena he demonstrates. "There is no traditional magician's perspective on extrasensory perception," he says. "I believe in telepathy and certain areas of clairvoyance. My departure from the general magician and the psychic is that I don't happen to believe that such phenomena are extrasensory. I believe they are based on heightened sensory awareness. Margaret Mead, the renowned anthropologist, is of the opinion that we have at least 22 senses. We all have senses that we take for granted like the sense of balance and the sense of pressure. I think that what might appear to be extrasensory perception can be answered in terms of these multiple senses on a subliminal level. That makes it less trickery in the magician's sense of the word but does not make it psychic. I argue with a magician who discounts parapsychology, but I also argue with the psychic who uses the phenomena to build a cult or claims to be a healer. I do not know what I should call myself. Mentalist is a show business term. But I would have to insist on being called a mentalist rather than a psychic or being credited with supernatural powers of any sort. My joke is that any child of seven could do what I do with 25 years of practice. I am conservative in an extravagant field."

THE AMAZING RANDI

Although The Amazing Randi is probably best known as an escape artist, he is proficient in all types of magic. Randi began as a magician's assistant, put together his own magic show, became a mentalist, dropped mentalism and concentrated on escapes. He had a radio show in New York City and is widely known as an author and personality in the magic field.

The first time Randi watched a friend perform a billiard-ball manipulation, he was captivated by magic. He haunted department stores buying tricks and learning to perform them. "When I was about thirteen, I heard about the Arcade Magic and Novelty Store in Toronto," he says. "Harry Smith owned the place. I was scared of him. He was tall and gaunt and had curly reddish hair and very heavy glasses. Harry asked me what I knew about magic, and I showed him the billiard-ball trick. He took the balls away from me and wouldn't let me do the trick that way again. Then, he showed me how it was supposed to be done.

"From that moment on I was an habitué of his store. Every Saturday afternoon all the kids my age would come in and stand around, making general nuisances of themselves. But Harry and his wife, Sophie, wouldn't have had it any other way.

1. The Amazing Randi undertakes an escape from a straitjacket while hanging upside down in mid-air. His assistants, Jim Pyczynski and Michael Chen, and a helpful spectator make sure the restraint is securely fastened.

"Then I met Terence Kingsley Lawson. T. K. Lawson was performing shows for 10 or 15 dollars a show. That was big money in those days. I began to work as his assistant. I never got paid much because T. K. would generally use whatever money he made to buy a corsage for his girl assistant. But we had great satisfaction. I remember one time when T. K. borrowed a .38 caliber revolver. We were performing in a beer parlor. T. K. was surrounded by drunks and the air was blue with smoke. 'No one sleeps while I work,' T. K. shouted and fired the revolver. The whole ceiling came down. Plaster dust was every place. We grabbed the props and ran for the exit while everybody laughed and applauded and spilled their beer."

Randi thanks magic for helping him overcome personal handicaps. "I was considered a child prodigy in school, and I found it uncomfortable," he

2. After the straitjacket is firmly in place, Randi's assistants fasten his feet in a frame which is in turn hooked to a crane.

3. Dangling upside down by his ankles, The Amazing Randi begins his ascent.

4. Fifty feet in the air, Randi struggles to release himself.

5. Randi flings the straitjacket aside. He has managed to liberate himself from the restraint in less than a minute.

says. "I didn't fit the system. I was a very retiring kid, and I stuttered and stammered. Performing magic helped me to get over that—it gave me the self-confidence I needed.

"At seventeen I left school and joined Peter March's traveling carnival. I was rained out and bitten by a lion and had all my props stolen. After that I became Prince Ibis with a turban and a suit of tails so moldy I could have grown potatoes in it. I did straight magic and worked up a mental act that went over well.

"By the time I was twenty I was the Great Randall, Telepath. I was heard across Canada on radio and was covered by the newspapers there. I was becoming well known as a so-called psychic. At the time I found it hard to believe that anyone would consider my feats the real thing. I thought I was putting on an act that they would temporarily

accept, then come to their senses and see it was trickery. But I found after a couple of stunts—once I predicted the outcome of the World Series correctly—my notoriety was so great people started to come to me for help in matters of health and for advice about the future. They thought I really was a psychic and had special powers. At that point I changed my name and left Toronto. That was in 1948. I came to the United States and later returned to Canada as The Amazing Randi."

Due partly to his early experience, Randi became a crusader against fraudulent psychics in the tradition of Harry Houdini and Joseph Dunninger. He believes there is no such thing as a psychic miracle. "For 30 years, I have been looking around the world for evidence of psychic phenomena," he says, "and I deny that any such thing exists. In every case I found a mistaken interpretation of

1. As a tribute to the Escape King, The Amazing Randi reenacts Houdini's suspenseful Milk Can Escape.

2. Climbing into the water-filled can, Randi seems barely able to squeeze himself into its cramped interior.

otherwise perfectly ordinary data or out-and-out skullduggery—simply cheating."

Randi's career as an escape artist invites comparisons with that of Harry Houdini, and parallels can be drawn. Escape artistry became Randi's profession almost in spite of himself. Like Houdini, Randi began doing jailbreaks for publicity. After some particularly newsworthy escapes, notably one from a jail in Quebec City, Quebec, people began to pressure him to concentrate on escapes. After a Chicago jailbreak, Houdini was similarly pressured by agent Martin Beck. Like Houdini, Randi found that it was necessary to combine magic with escapery to fill a show, but his escapes continued to draw the best press coverage. In some ways Randi regrets his decision. "At that point I began walking in the shadow of Harry Houdini, and I have not been able to get out of it since," he says. "It was a mistake, but it was a mistake that was almost thrust upon me. I never claimed to be another Houdini. I never even said that I imitated him. The comparison is not a bad thing to be saddled with, but you can never quite be Houdini and if you seem to be imitating him, you are only an imitator and that's bad."

Naturally, there is some overlap in the stunts performed by Randi and Houdini. Occasionally, Randi stages a faithful duplication of one of the Escape King's releases (with full credit to the creator). Randi has escaped from ropes, handcuffs, boxes and coffins. He performs the Hanging Straitjacket Escape and continues to stage jailbreaks. But Randi's style is very much his own. Major escapes, such as from a locked milk can filled with water, are very dramatic, but Randi uses a lighthearted style when performing simpler releases and straight magic. He jokes while he performs a rope release. "I don't tell my mother what I do for a living," he tells the audience. "She thinks I sell dope." When he does the Torn-and-Restored Newspaper trick, his monologue befits a stand-up comedian. If he does his version of Blackstone's Sawing-a-Woman-in-Half stunt in full view with a buzz saw, he pans it. His version is funny instead of frightening. Randi is equally at ease as a master of ceremonies or as a magician at a children's show. "But I won't do something like the buzz saw for children," he says. "Even in fun it could upset them."

3. Randi's assistants, Jim Pyczynski and Bob Dezort, pour additional water into the can to make certain there is no air space.

4. Football stars Joe Greene and Franco Harris assist in forcing the lid onto the can.

Randi stresses that his escapes are not death defying. "An escape artist beats the odds like a mentalist," he says. "You're not likely to be able to get out of a straitjacket or a can full of water. It does take a bit of derring-do and intestinal fortitude to do some of the things I do. A lot of people would be terrified at the idea of hanging upside down 100 feet in the air. It doesn't bother me because I know I am as safe as if I were home in bed."

Randi is particularly careful in selecting assistants. "My assistants have to be able to think on their own or they are no help to me in an emergency," he says. "I need to have someone with me that I can fully trust." In a way, Randi's assistants are more apprentices than helpers. Jim Pyczynski, for instance, who acted as Randi's assistant from 1974 to 1976, was in the process of establishing himself as a magician and escape artist while working with Randi.

Besides competent assistance, Randi's own mechanical expertise is the factor that most often prevents catastrophe. For example, the frame he uses when performing his Hanging Straitjacket Escape has been tested and retested. It is constructed in such a way that three separate mechanisms work independently. If one fails, the others will hold him. Randi, of course, has a thorough knowledge of every sort of lock, and he also builds his own equipment for his regular magic shows.

In spite of his precautions, Randi has occasion-ally found himself in danger. Once he was locked inside a safe when he realized the mechanism was rigged so that if he tripped it incorrectly, he could be locked inside permanently. He finally called for help as he was about to run out of air. His assistant, Moses Figueroa, was standing by and knew how to release him. "If I had realized the devices were there," says Randi, "I never would have tried the escape. You can still do dumb things no matter how long you have been in the business. When that happens, I have to apologize to my audience for having done a stupid thing."

Randi has made three tours of Europe and two around the world. "Working in other countries puts me in close touch with my profession of being a magician," he says. "In some ways it is more rewarding to work before people who do not speak your language. I practice my art with more skill when I can't rely on verbal communication.

"It's a strange profession but it's not that far removed from acting. A magician is a part that I play. I could have chosen another. How convincingly I play my part depends entirely on my acting ability and my ability to produce the effect I want with the equipment, the motions—sleight of hand, if you will—and my conviction as an actor. Of course, I'd like to be remembered. I'd like someone to get up on stage some day and say that he or she became interested in magic because of a performance by The Amazing Randi. But I'd like to be known as a person, too, not just as some strange character who puts on the mask of a magician."

5. The cover of the milk can is fastened by a half-dozen padlocks supplied and inspected by a local locksmith.

6. As the seconds tick by, tension in the theater mounts. Randi's assistants stand by in case of accident.

7. Two and one half minutes after being locked inside, Randi emerges. His faithful presentation of the stunt includes Bob Dezort's rendition of the original organ accompaniment—**Asleep in the Deep**.

The World's Greatest Magic Secrets

(PLUS MAGIC YOU, TOO, CAN DO)

Tricks compiled and performed by The Amazing Randi.
Written by Catherine Cashion.
Edited by Nancy Naglin. Designed by Rochelle Arthur Lapidus and Patricia Lee.
Illustrated by Sally Shimizu. Photographed by Paul Levin.

The Overturning Coin

The magician announces that he will try to flip a coin from tails to heads while it is under a saltshaker. Suddenly the saltshaker itself vanishes. As the magician wonders aloud what went wrong, he feels something in the sleeve of his jacket. He reaches in to discover the missing saltshaker. This trick illustrates one of the basic principles of the magic art, that of misdirection. The trick's title and the magician's stated purpose focus audience attention on the coin, which actually has nothing to do with the trick.

Preparation: This is an impromptu trick, effectively performed quite casually at the dinner table. The only props you need are a large coin, a saltshaker, and two paper napkins.

l. Start by telling your audience that you have an ordinary quarter, placed heads down.

2. "While it is covered with this saltshaker," you say, "I will attempt to use my magical skills to turn the quarter over so it is heads up. I will not touch the quarter."

3. "To assure you that I will not slip the coin from under the saltshaker, I will cover the shaker with paper napkins."

4. Show the audience that the napkins contain no secret holes or hems and lay them at right angles over the saltshaker.

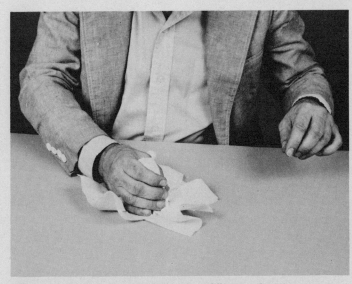

5. As you utter magic words in the hope of flipping the coin over, grasp the saltshaker, shaping the paper napkins around it.

6. As you check to see if the trick has worked, slide the covered salt-shaker to the edge of the table and drop the shaker into your lap. Move slowly so as not to distract attention away from the coin.

7. "Heads are still down. I'll have to try again." Place the empty but still shaped napkins over the coin, being careful to maintain the shaker shape.

8. Suddenly crush the paper napkins to reveal to the audience for the first time that the saltshaker is missing.

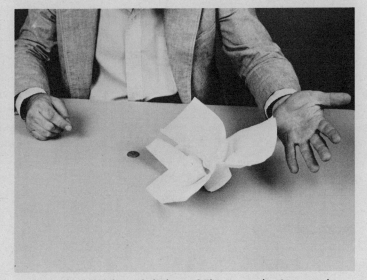

9. "Hey, where did that saltshaker go? This is not what I expected. The coin was supposed to turn over."

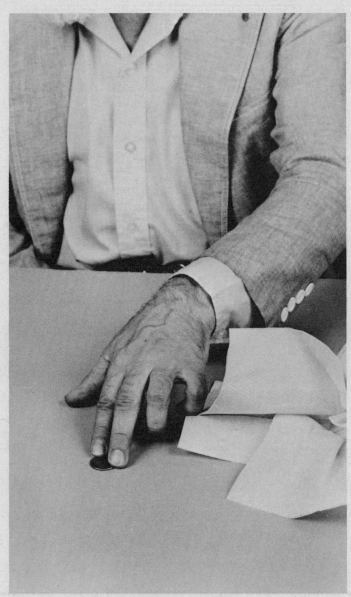

10. As you push the coin forward to show the audience your failure, move your other hand back into your lap to retrieve the saltshaker. The double motion makes this essential action go unnoticed.

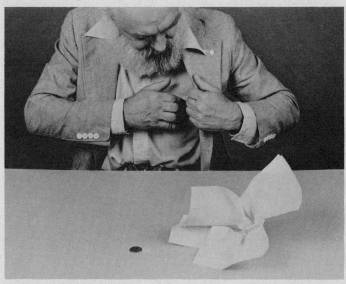

11. It is important that you account for the lost saltshaker. With it hidden in your hand, move that hand toward the inside of your jacket.

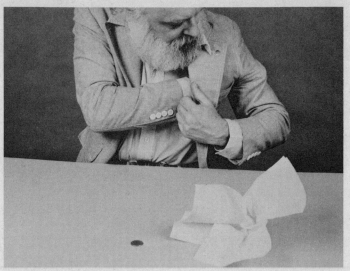

12. "Wait a minute, what's this I feel? Something is crawling up my arm." Reach deep into your sleeve pressing the saltshaker so its shape is apparent through the coat.

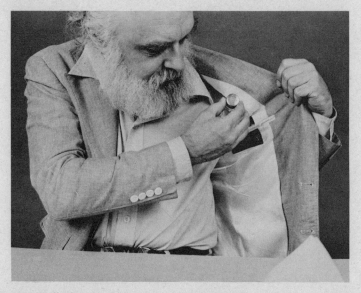

13. "Well what do you know—here's the little rascal."

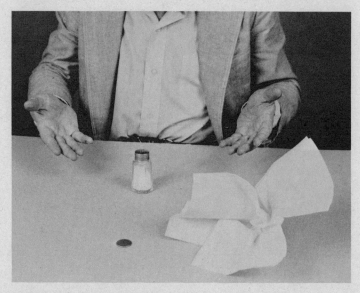

14. The audience has been treated to a trick it didn't expect.

An Impossible Prediction

The magician takes a handful of change from his pocket and chooses several coins, which he places in a spectator's hand. He immediately closes the hand so the volunteer will have no idea of how many coins the magician has given him. The magician asks the volunteer to choose a number but keep it secret. Then he leads the recruit through a series of arithmetical calculations. At the end of this exercise, the magician tells the volunteer that the number he has reached in his head is the exact number of coins he is holding in his hand. The volunteer is gleeful because the formula has led him to number two and a half. Believing there is no such thing as a half coin, he thinks he has bested the magician. To his surprise, when he opens his hand there are two and a half coins in his palm.

Preparation: You must neatly saw a coin in half, and put one half in your pocket with the rest of your change. When you secretly choose the coins at the start of the trick, select the half coin and two other coins, preferably all of one denomination.

The mathematical formula which effects the trick is credited to Sam Dalal, an Indian magician, and is as follows: the volunteer chooses any number at all, for example 20. You then ask him to add the next highest number (in this case 21), and then to add 9. This sum (50) must then be divided in half. From the new answer (25), the original number is subtracted. At this point in the calculations, your volunteer will have the number 5 in his head. Then when you ask him to divide this number exactly in half, he will think you have made a mistake. This ensures a startling conclusion to a foolproof trick.

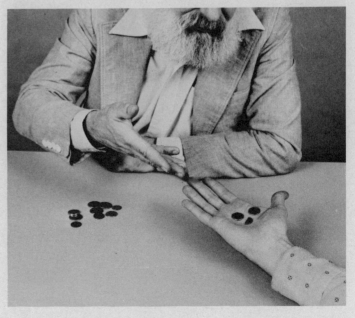

In mathematical terms, the formula you must memorize is: $[(n) + (n + 1) + 9] \div 2 \times (2n + 10) \div 2 = (n + 5)$, and $(n + 5) - n = 5$ which, when divided by 2, equals $2\frac{1}{2}$. The formula makes obvious the fact that the trick will work with any number. However, most people, when performing your step-by-step demands, will not realize that the calculations always lead to $2\frac{1}{2}$. The volunteer's freedom to choose any number, after you have hidden the coins, seems to imply a magical prediction.

173

The Lady and the Phoenix

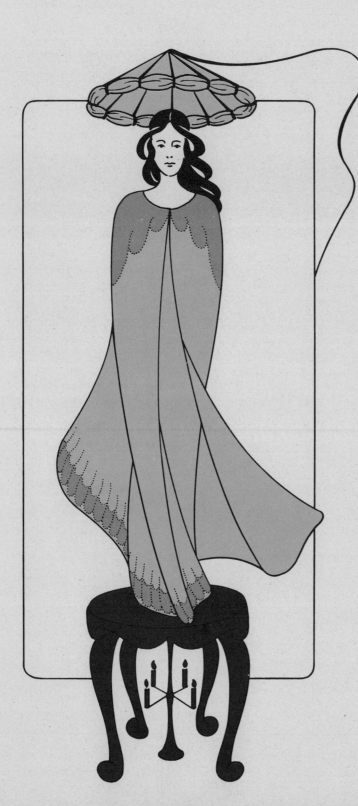

A young woman stands on top of a light, four-legged table surrounded on three sides by a hinged screen. Above her is gathered a cylindrical curtain which can be raised or lowered with a drawstring. Under the table are four burning candles in a candelabrum. The magician drops the curtain, which completely conceals the woman, and invites spectators to stand outside the partition, precluding an exit through the back screen. When he fires a pistol, smoke and flames pour from within the curtain. Seconds later, the magician raises the curtain to reveal a magical bird rising from a cloud of smoke.

This trick, first performed in 1892, was inspired by H. Rider Haggard's best-selling novel, **She,** in which a beautiful African queen had mysteriously lived more than 2,000 years and suddenly turned into a pile of skin and bones before the eyes of her astonished companions. The bizarre novel was so widely read that the illusion, originally employing even the skull and bones, generated great excitement. Obviously, the illusion is engineered behind the curtain, but how?

The space under the table seems to be open, and the four burning candles reinforce this illusion. Actually, the table is built into a triangular box covered with mirrors. Two vertical mirrors, projecting at 45-degree angles from the back edges of the screen, meet at the central rod of the candelabrum and so go unnoticed. The table actually has only two legs and only two candles burn beneath it; the other two legs and candles are reflections in the mirrors. Since the side and back screens are the same color, these mirrors, reflecting the side panels, create the illusion that observers are looking under the table to the back screen. A horizontal mirror at table height, which extends behind the table top and forms the top of the triangular box, also reflects the back panel.

When the woman is covered with the curtain, she can easily go through a trap door in the table top, climbing down into the triangular box. Viewers believe they will see her the moment she steps off the table top. Before she disappears through the trap door, she plants the bird and the fireworks which will simulate her reincarnation.

The mysterious woman, rein-
carnated as a beautiful bird
under the magician's spell,
peers silently at the incredu-
lous audience through clouds
of smoke.

Walking Through a Brick Wall

Ever since Harry Houdini first performed the trick at the New York Hippodrome, walking through a brick wall has been thought by many to be a perfect, foolproof illusion. The most keen eyed of observers cannot spot the fakery they know must be involved. The magician invites a committee of audience volunteers on stage to watch the proceedings. First, they inspect the large, heavy rug that covers the stage. Its unvarying color and texture would make any open seam or slit quite obvious. Then, the magician brings out a smaller cloth for the committee to lay over the rug in order to reinforce its impenetrability.

Bricklayers arrive on stage and begin laying bricks in mortar in routine fashion. The observers examine the bricks and watch as a wall is built on an iron beam with casters for the sake of mobility. Work continues until the wall is 10 feet high and 12 feet long. When the wall is completed, it is rolled to center stage. The audience, viewing one end of the wall, can see that it is a foot thick. The volunteers on stage circle it.

A three-section hinged screen is placed tight against either side of the wall to conceal the actual execution. Since the screens are only large enough to hide a man, the wall is visible above them and beside them in both directions. The magician slips behind the screen on one side of the wall. Within 30 seconds he pushes away the screen on the other side and walks out on stage to join the group of stupefied observers. Everyone is certain the wall contains no secret passage and that the solid rugs prevent an escape through a trap door underneath.

As a matter of fact, this trick does make clever use of the trap door. As is always the case with magic, things are not positioned as casually as they seem to be. Double trap doors lie directly beneath the screened-off area, one on each side of the wall. These are opened by a stage hand as soon as the magician moves behind the screen. When the stage floor is dropped, the rug above sags just enough to allow any agile man to slip under the wall through the tunnel provided by the slack. The volunteers who stand on the edges of the rug unknowingly aid the illusion by forcing the rug to stretch rather than slide into the space provided by the open trap door. Once the magician has passed under the wall, the trap doors are closed again and the rug springs back to its original shape.

The Transposed Cup of Water

The magician fills a cup with water, places it momentarily inside a hat, then moves it from the hat to a paper bag. When he crumples the paper bag, there is no sign of spilled water. The cup with water is found inside the hat.

Preparation: Carefully cut the top rim and the bottom from a paper cup, making a "shell" of the same size and design as the other two cups used in the trick.

1. "I have here two paper cups, one full of water and the other empty," you tell the audience.

2. Actually, you have concealed the bottomless paper shell inside the empty cup before the trick begins.

3. "Now I'll pour all the water, from one cup to the other." Be sure to keep the shell from bobbing up as the water flows in.

4. "I can choose to put the cup of water in the hat or in the paper bag." First lower the full cup into the hat.

5. "Since I'm in charge, I opt for the paper bag." You actually remove only the paper shell, leaving the full cup of water in the hat.

6. Handling the shell as though it were a cup full of water, transfer it as quickly as possible to the paper bag, hiding its bottomless state.

7. Now lift the bag very gently to reinforce the illusion that you are trying not to spill the water inside.

8. Quite unexpectedly, crush the bag into a small ball and toss it over your shoulder.

9. "And where did our cup of water go?" you ask. "By some strange means, it has been spirited over to the hat."

10. Pour the water from this cup back into the cup originally filled and pass both of them to the audience for their inspection.

179

The "Psychic" Key Bend

A person of average strength can bend keys easily by either of the two following methods. This is not common knowledge because most people never try to bend their keys. (Remember that bent keys will not work in the locks for which they were made.)

Preparation—first method: Select the keys carefully. Brass and aluminum keys are more easily bent than steel. At least one key must have an oblong slot in its head, rather than the usual small hole. This slotted key will serve as a tool for bending.

1. After removing two keys from a volunteer's key ring, show the audience that both keys are flat at the outset.

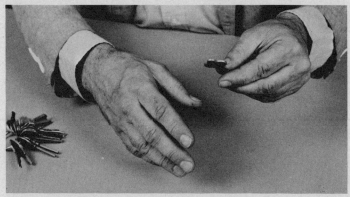

2. Hook the end of one key through the slot in the other. The slot serves as a fulcrum which you can use to gain leverage in bending the key.

3. As you hide this mechanical set-up with your hand, talk with the volunteer who will take the keys.

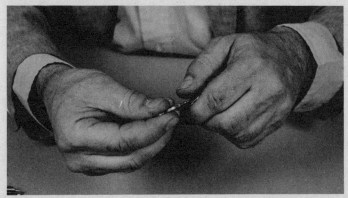

4. As you talk to the volunteer, establishing eye-to-eye contact and distracting attention from your hands, press the top key forward sharply with your thumb, thereby producing a bend.

5. With your thumb, cover the bend as you casually disengage the keys. As is often the case with magic, you have accomplished the trick before it even seems to have begun.

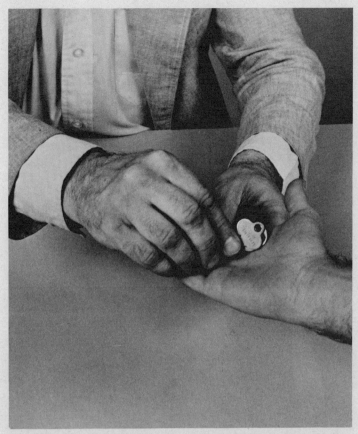

6. Place the keys in the volunteer's hand, and curl his fingers quickly over them.

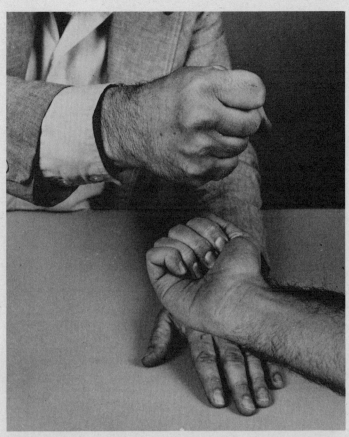

7. With your fist held over the volunteer's, intone three times, "Bend, bend, bend."

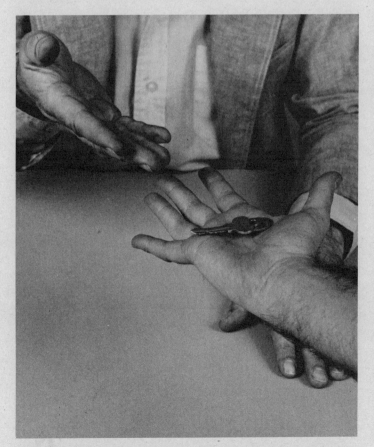

8. When the volunteer opens his hand, one of his keys is bent. Although the trick seems supernatural, it consists of a simple application of basic physics.

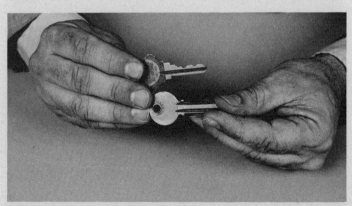

9. **Preparation—second method:** This trick can also be done with a single key. A key with a deep cut near the center is ideal (top).

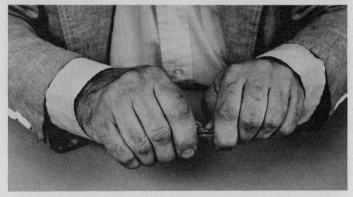

10. You can bend the key by suddenly applying heavy pressure with the thumbs. As you do this, turn away from the audience under the pretense of looking for better light or some such ploy.

The Blue-Room Illusion

The magician invites a volunteer from the audience to stand inside the "blue room"— a three-sided, midnight-blue box positioned vertically at the back of the stage. The open side of the box faces the audience. A black velvet drapery covers the walls surrounding the stage. When the magician commands the illusion to begin, the body of the person in the box slowly dissolves into a skeleton. Then, at the magician's word, the skeleton gradually disappears and the body is fully restored. The volunteer walks out of the blue room, suffering no apparent trauma and very much alive.

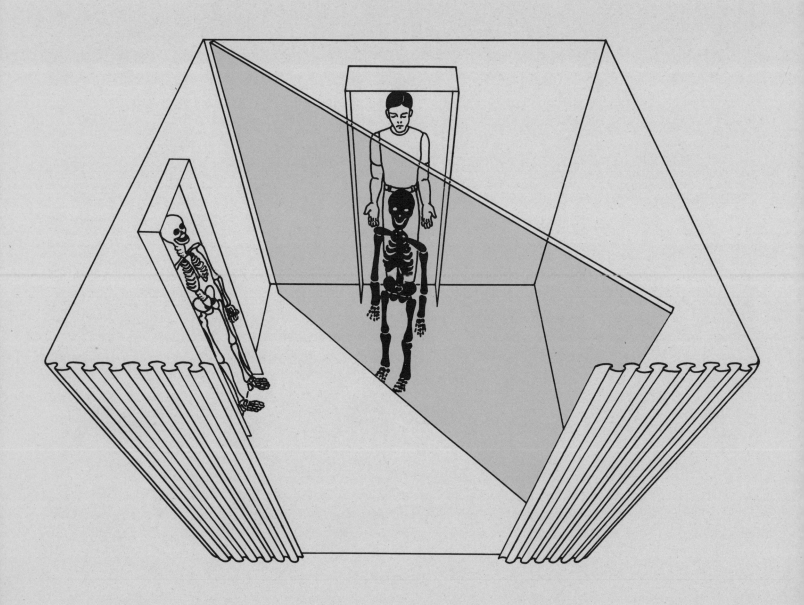

Conjurers have manipulated ghost figures for centuries. In the Middle Ages, magicians caused magnified images to appear in clouds of smoke, probably by means of mirrors and lenses similar in principle to those of a modern slide projector. Sharper three-dimensional images became popular after 1863, when a Professor Pepper of the London Polytechnic Institute began using the reflective properties of clear glass to perform spectral illusions. The blue-room illusion, a part of this tradition, is a basic experiment with the physical properties of light.

Careful technical arrangements make the trick work. Offstage at one side is another blue room, identical with the one containing the volunteer from the audience. In this hidden room is a skeleton. Powerful sets of lights are directed at each box. Also invisible to the audience is a large sheet of glass which cuts across the stage at a 45-degree angle. The edges of the glass are hidden by the curtains. The trick is based on the principle that by reflecting light it is possible to make hidden things visible.

As the illusion begins, the person in the blue room is brightly illuminated. The audience can see him through the glass without suspecting the presence of the glass. At the magician's command, the lights focused on the man are slowly dimmed as other lights aimed at the skeleton offstage are brightened. As less light strikes the man in the box, he becomes less visible to the audience. As more light reflected from the skeleton strikes the glass, the image of the skeleton is reflected—and people begin to see the skeleton. The angle of the glass and the placement of the two blue rooms are such that the image of the skeleton appears at the same point as the audience sees the man in the box. Thus the man's body seems to be replaced by the skeleton.

The image of the skeleton reflected from the glass is actually rather dim. For it to appear relatively bright and sharp, the rest of the stage must be quite dark. The black drapery surrounding the stage aids the illusion by absorbing random light which might otherwise distract the eye from the spectral figure. Smoking must be prohibited in the hall because clear air ensures a clearly reflected image.

The man in the blue room feels nothing out of the ordinary and can only wonder at the astonished reaction of the audience.

Ropes Through the Neck

The magician takes two pieces of soft rope, each about four feet long, and ties them around his neck. Then, with a very quick, strong jerk, he seems to pull the ropes through his neck, although the painless expression on his face assures the audience that magic is involved.

Preparation: Tie the two lengths of rope together, side by side, at their midway point, using a thin piece of white thread. Avoid using nylon or other type of very strong thread, since it must be easy to break. This small thread will fall to the floor unnoticed when it is snapped in two by the magician.

1. Show the audience the two pieces of rope, holding them close together to conceal the place where the ropes are joined with thread.

2. Let the ropes drop into one hand, so that all four ends hang closely together from the spot where the thread is tied.

3. With the ropes in this position, place your finger and thumb between them, without letting the audience see you do so.

4. This results in one entire rope falling on each side of the thread tie, rather than each rope extending in both directions from this point.

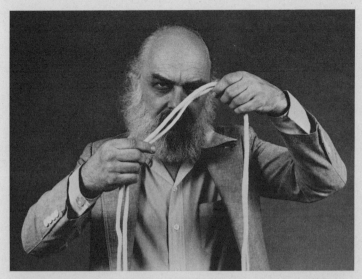

5. With your hand covering the thread tie, put the ropes around your head. Do this casually and the audience will not suspect that the ropes are no longer parallel.

6. "Let's tie these ropes around my neck with a double knot," you say. "Then there will be no possibility that I can slip them over my head while you're not looking."

7. "Would two spectators be so kind as to pull the ends of the rope taut to tighten up the knot for me?" Represent all this emphasis on the knot as security against fakery for the audience's sake. Actually, the knot is essential to the illusion's success.

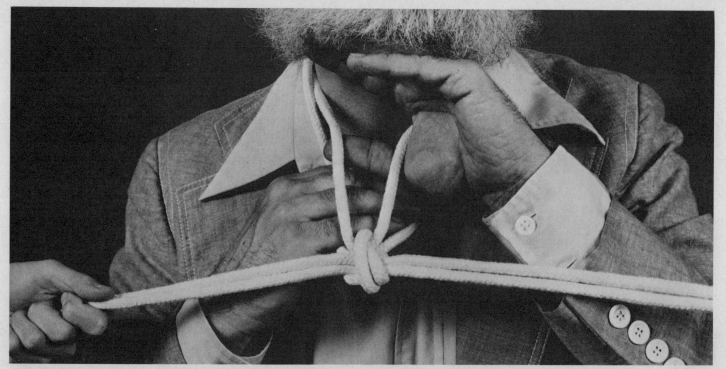

8. The way you hold the ropes at this point is essential to the illusion. Rather than grasping the doubled rope on either side of the neck, hold the top two ropes from the right and left sides of the neck in one fist and the bottom two ropes in the other.

9. If you keep both fists very close together at the throat, you can conceal the crisscrossing ropes which result from the special hold.

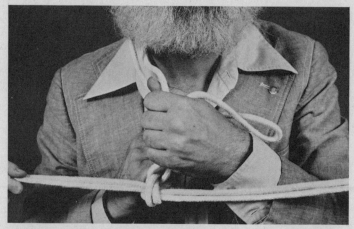

10. Give the ropes a sudden hard jerk, snapping the weak thread binding them together at the back of the neck.

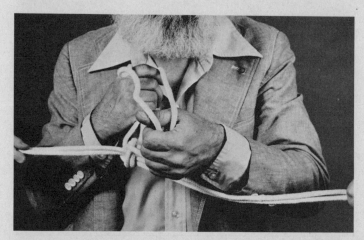

11. As the curves at the middle of each rope fall forward, quickly rotate your hands, pulling the ropes into a tight circle to keep the audience from detecting your method.

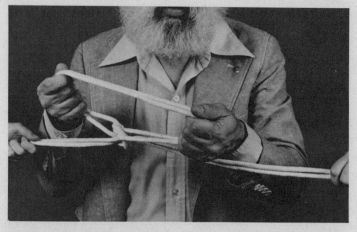

12. The circle now seems to have been the one that was around your neck. After unknotting the ropes, thereby destroying the remaining evidence of the trick's modus operandi, let the audience examine them.

The Eyeless Vision Trick

To do this trick, borrow an ordinary bandanna handkerchief from someone in the audience. If you fold it elaborately and tie it across your eyes, there will appear to be a very thick layer of material obscuring your vision. In reality, you will have pleated both ends of the bandanna toward the center, without ever actually reaching it. Therefore, along the narrow gap in the middle of the kerchief, there will be only a single layer of cloth, through which you can easily see.

Taking bills of various denominations from audience members, pretend to decipher the serial numbers with your fingertips. Actually, you will be reading them easily through your transparent blindfold.

A

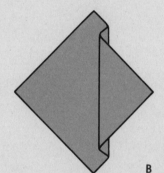

B

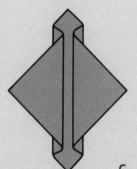

C

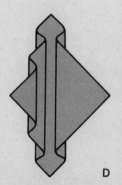

D

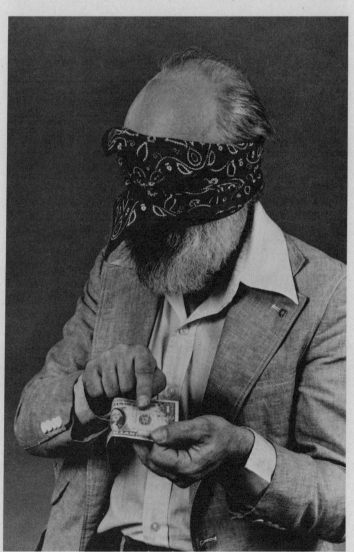

A Prophetic Card Trick

The magician fans out a deck of cards, faces down, to show that it is a legitimate deck. Then he hands the deck to a volunteer from the audience and gives the following instructions: "Place the deck behind your back, then remove the top card from the pack and insert it somewhere in the middle of the pack. That was easy, wasn't it? Now do the same with the next card, but turn it over before inserting it in the pack. That card will be easy to find, won't it? It will be the only card turned faceup in the deck. Now cut the deck as many times as you like. Before you hand the cards back to me, I want to ask you a question. Is it possible for you to know what card is now face to face with the card you turned over in the pack? Of course not. I am going to predict at what point in the deck you have inserted the upside-down card. I'm going to say that your card is lying face to face with the two of spades. Now spread the deck on the table and let's see. Yes, there's your card. What card is above your card? Why, it's the two of spades."

Preparation: To do this trick, you must prepare cards without letting the volunteer know you have done so. Turn over the second card from the top of the deck and the second card from the bottom, so they are faceup in the pack. The back of the cards should have a white border so the overturned cards are not noticeable, even if the pack is fanned slightly. You must memorize the **third card from the bottom**, for this is the card you will predict.

When you fan the cards for the audience, be careful not to reveal the turned cards—leave a few cards near the top and bottom unfanned. Then, as the volunteer follows your instructions, he actually will reverse the second card from the top and place it into the middle of the deck. This move restores it to a facedown position, and leaves only a single card turned faceup in the deck—the card you placed faceup near the bottom of the pack during your initial preparation. After a few cuts this will appear to be the card the volunteer turned over and inserted.

By cutting the cards, the volunteer does not change their order—the overturned card remains next to the card you have memorized. You should insist on at least two or three cuts of the deck; the overturned card would appear suspiciously near the center of the deck after a single cut.

In the unlikely event (one chance in 52) that the volunteer will cut between these two cards, then, quickly spotting the overturned card on the top of the deck, you can improvise a double miracle, since your prediction is now at the bottom of the pack. "Now you'll notice that by a strange coincidence, you have cut the deck at the exact point where your card is overturned," you say. "That means that not only was I able to predict the point at which you inserted the upside-down card, but in spite of the fact that you made as many cuts as you wanted, you were forced to make the final cut at the point precisely between those two cards."

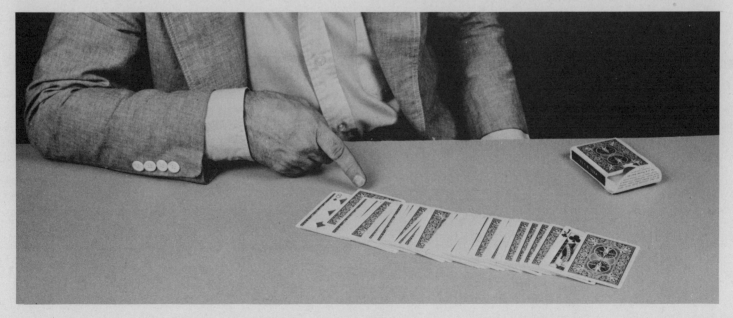

Escape From a Pillory

The magician is securely tied to her pillory. The detail shows the left wrist rope before it is tied. When the rope is threaded through its holes, it is caught by a hidden loop in the mechanism inside the wood.

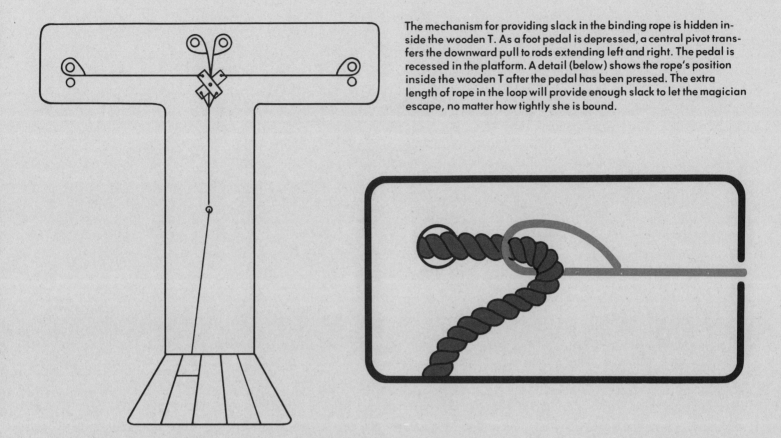

The mechanism for providing slack in the binding rope is hidden inside the wooden T. As a foot pedal is depressed, a central pivot transfers the downward pull to rods extending left and right. The pedal is recessed in the platform. A detail (below) shows the rope's position inside the wooden T after the pedal has been pressed. The extra length of rope in the loop will provide enough slack to let the magician escape, no matter how tightly she is bound.

A wooden T-shaped structure about the height of a man is mounted on a small platform. At three places along the crossbar are ropes threaded through pairs of holes with the ends hanging in front of the bar. The magician invites a volunteer from the audience to tie her to the pillory. Usually she asks for a sailor or some other person skilled in knot-tying techniques. The ropes are heavy but flexible enough to move easily through the holes in the wood; the structure seems solid and heavy.

The magician steps onto the platform and stands with her back against the wooden T and her arms outstretched. As the audience watches, the volunteer ties the arms and neck of the magician to the pillory with elaborate knots, which he then seals with wax provided by an assistant. The wax is marked with the impression of a key from the volunteer's pocket. A large screen is then placed in front of the magician.

As a drum begins to roll, the magician instantly pushes away the screen to reveal herself freed from her bonds. The ropes remain tightly knotted and sealed. The magician cuts the ropes free and throws them to the audience for inspection.

It seems such an escape would require miraculously contractible wrists and neck, but the magician has relied instead on a mechanical aid. A slot in the T conceals four iron rods, each looped at the end. There is one loop for each wrist rope and two for the neck rope. All are connected to a hidden central rod which runs down the T to a foot pedal in the platform. The pedal goes unnoticed because attention is focused on the ropes.

When the magician mounts the platform, he steps on the pedal. By means of a spring, the pedal pulls all of the rods toward itself. The loops catch the ropes and pull on them, providing the slack needed for the later escape. As long as the magician has her foot on the pedal, the ropes bind her tightly. When she is hidden by the screen, she removes her foot from the pedal, letting the rope loosen enough so she can easily slide her hands and head out without disturbing a single knot.

The Cut-and-Restored Newspaper Strip

This simple but mystifying trick was often performed on stage by Harry Blackstone, Sr. The magician showed the audience a long strip of newspaper, which he folded in half. Using scissors, he cut off the folded edge. Then, grasping one of the loose ends, he quickly unfolded the column to reveal the strip in one piece, but slightly shortened. If you do this trick for an audience, repeat it several times, so you appear to restore the strip miraculously after each cut until the column becomes quite short.

Preparation: Coat the strip of newspaper heavily on one side with paper-type rubber cement. After the cement has dried thoroughly (for at least ten minutes), dust it lightly with talcum powder to prevent the surface from sticking to itself when the strip is folded in half during the performance.

1. Show the audience the prepared strip of newspaper, proclaiming it to be quite ordinary.

2. Fold the paper so the prepared surface meets itself, and make a sharp crease with your thumbnail.

3. Using a pair of sharp scissors, make a straight cut just below the folded edge.

4. Crumple the cut-off piece of the column's center and with reckless abandon cast it away.

5. Miraculously, the strip is restored! Actually, the thin edges of rubber cement, exposed by the cut, adhere to each other to form a joint.

6. Repeat the cut several times, being careful always to fold the paper with the rubber cement on the inside.

7. Before the very eyes of the audience, the strip will grow shorter with each snip of the scissors.

8. Although the joints are weak, if you handle the paper carefully they will hold throughout the performance of the trick.

9. On the last cut, pretend to slip, and cut the paper at an angle. Actually, you want to cut it accurately at a 45-degree angle.

10. The paper survives even your apparent clumsiness, remaining in one piece.

The Magazine Mind-Reading Miracle

The magician boasts that he will perform an act of mind reading. Audience members shudder at the realization that he may already be seeing their thoughts clearly. Finding a volunteer for this trick is difficult until the magician clarifies the trick's domain. He will read only the objective facts which a volunteer will glean from the pages of a magazine. The volunteer is invited to select any one page from any of the various magazine issues that lie on the table. When the volunteer closes his magazine, the magician is able to tell him all about the page on which he has been concentrating. Photographs on the page are accurately described and the first few printed lines are quoted exactly.

Preparation: You will need several copies of the same issue of a magazine to do this trick. Remove their covers and paste the covers of different issues of the same magazine in their place.

1. "Choose any magazine and see what the last page number in that issue is; then pick any number between one and that number and tell me what it is," you tell the volunteer. Pick up what appears to be a different issue of the magazine, simply to demonstrate to the volunteer what you want done.

2. "Now turn to the page number you have selected but hold the magazine upright like this so I can't see the page." You have estimated where the selected page will be in your identical copy of the magazine. While you show the volunteer how to hold the magazine, see how far from the right page number you are.

3. "I want you to concentrate very hard on your page, making a note of all its prominent features." While talking to the volunteer, lay your magazine on the table and thumb the pages forward or backward until by counting you arrive surreptitiously at the same page the volunteer is studying.

4. "Hold your magazine high in front of your face like this, so there will be no chance that I can catch a glimpse of your page." As you show the volunteer the safe way to position his magazine, study the same page yourself, quickly absorbing enough information to startle the spectator when his magazine is closed.

Disappearance
of a Horse and Rider

A beautifully costumed rider maneuvers a handsome, high-spirited horse onto the stage. The horse's white coat, highlighted by a decorative harness, contrasts dramatically with the heavy drapery of black velvet hanging sumptuously around the stage. The horse walks up an inclined plane to a large horizontal platform supported by two trestles. The walkway is removed and the horse with its rider stands elevated above the stage in full view of the audience. From above, a curtain pole is lowered by means of chains attached to each end until it is in front of and just above the horse and rider.

The magician pulls down a brightly colored shade from the roller to conceal horse and rider from view. Within seconds he snaps the blind back up, and they are gone. Stagehands carry off the trestles and platform. The curtain rod is raised above the stage. No trace of horse or rider remains.

The horse and rider could not have escaped through a trap door. The audience can see the stage floor under the platform, and a horse could not get down from the platform without quite a clatter. The horse certainly was not rolled up in the shade.

Actually, the horse and rider were hoisted above the stage without the audience's knowledge. The roller blind attached to the chains effects the illusion. A spectator in the audience believes he can see between the chains to the back of the stage. He thinks the only space hidden is the one directly behind the roller shade covering the horse. He does not consider the possibility of the horse being lifted. The flimsiness of the shade enhances his confidence that he can detect any movement behind it.

But black velvet, identical with the backdrop material, fills the space between the chains and blocks the audience's view. As soon as the colored shade is drawn in front of the horse, cables drop from above and are hooked by the rider to the specially designed harness. The cables run over sets of pulleys, and are connected to a windlass cranked by stagehands offstage. By the time the blind is snapped up, the horse has been raised aloft and is hidden by the black velvet curtain.

In this illusion lighting plays a role in fooling the audience. The stage seems brightly lit, but all the illumination comes from the front of the stage and the footlights. All overhead lights are turned off, making it impossible to distinguish the black velvet curtain between the chains from the stage's black backdrop.

From the wings of the stage, the disappearing horse and rider can be seen, hoisted high above the thin roller blind. Their ascent is now hidden from the audience by the invisible black velvet stretched between the chains.

The Dematerializing Coin

The magician folds a large coin inside a piece of paper until it seems completely wrapped. He lays the packet on the table and asks a spectator to put his hand over it. After uttering a magic word, the magician moves the spectator's hand and tears the folded paper in half. The coin is no longer inside.

Preparation: You will need a square piece of paper much larger than the coin for this trick, plus the coin itself and a drinking glass.

1. "Here I have a silver dollar, which I will fold up inside this sheet of paper," you say.

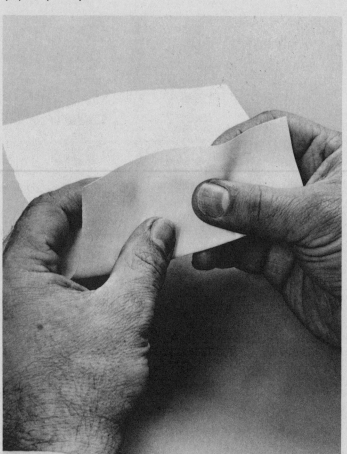

2. Hold the coin in the center of the sheet and fold the bottom third of the paper over it.

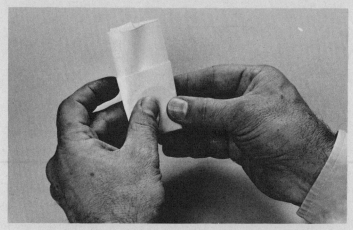

3. Fold the left and right sides of the paper toward the spectator, covering the coin.

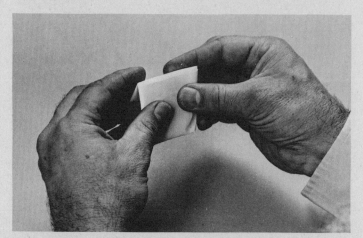

4. Fold the top half of the packet toward the spectator so the coin seems to be completely enclosed.

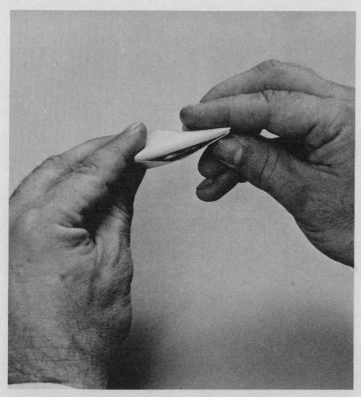

5. Actually, you have saved an open pocket through which the coin can escape.

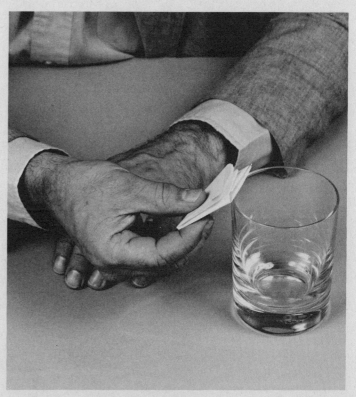

6. "The coin is completely wrapped in this paper," you say. "You can hear it when I rap it against this glass."

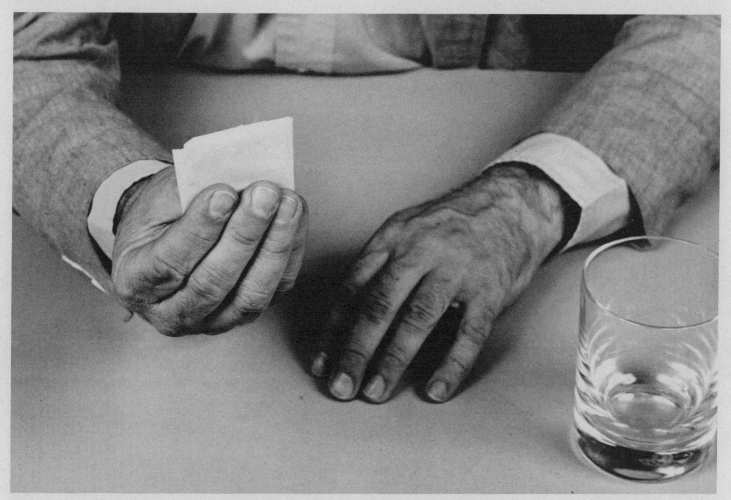

7. As you move the folded paper to the glass, rotate it toward you so the open end of the pocket points downward, and wrap your fingers around the pocket. You can hold the coin in the up-side down pocket by applying pressure with your thumb.

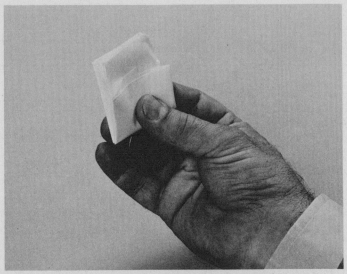

8. As you hold the packet up for the audience to see, let the coin slip into your hand where you can hold it until you find it convenient to drop it into your coat pocket.

9. Hold the now empty packet on the table with one finger to prevent the slight unfolding which might reveal the absence of the coin's weight within.

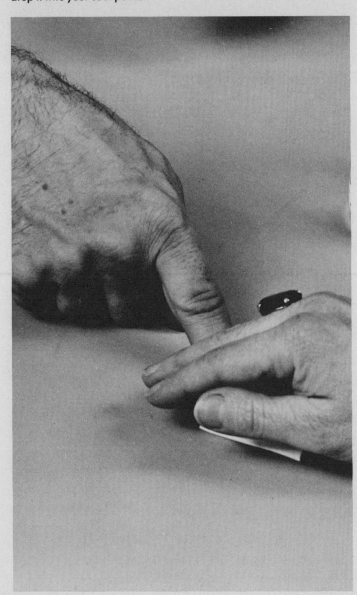

10. "Will you please cup your hand over the coin while I speak the magic charm?"

11. "Thank you very much. Let's tear into this packet and see if the spell has worked."

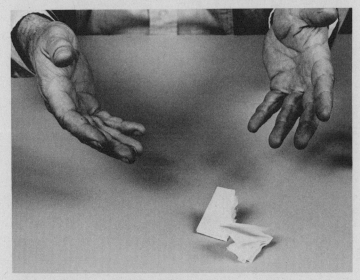

12. "Yes, the coin seems to have vanished. With results like this, who needs magical powers, anyway?"

BIBLIOGRAPHY

The Origins and History of Magic

Allusions to Witchcraft and Other Primitive Beliefs in the Zoroastroan Literature. Leo Joachim Frachtenberg. Fort Printing Press, Bombay, India

Annals of Conjuring, The. Sidney Wrangel Clarke. George Johnson, London, England

Ancient Art and Ritual. Jane Ellen Harrison. H. Holt and Co., New York

Bulfinch's Mythology. Thomas Bulfinch. The Modern Library (Random House), New York

Discoverie of Witchcraft, The. Reginald Scot. William Brome, London, England

Forge and the Crucible, The. Mircea Eliade. Harper and Row, New York and Evanston

History of Magic and Experimental Science, A. Lynn Thorndike. Macmillan Co., Inc., New York

History of Playing Cards, A. Catherine Perry Hargrave. Dover Publications, New York

Illustrated History of Magic, The. Milbourne Christopher. Thomas Y. Crowell Co., New York

Japanese Mythology. Juliet Piggott. The Hamlyn Publishing Group, Ltd., Feltham, Middlesex, England

Life of Merlin, Surnamed Ambrosius, The. Thomas Heywood. Lackington Allen and Co., London, England

Lives of the Conjurers, The. Thomas Frost. Chatto and Windus, London, England

Lives of the Necromancers. William Godwin. F. J. Mason, London, England

Mediaeval Magic. Robert Steele. Quarterly Review, Volume 240, New York

Myth of the Magus, The. Eliza Marian Butler. University Press, Cambridge, England

Mythology of all Races, The, Volume VIII (Chinese Mythology, John C. Ferguson; Japanese Mythology, Masaharu Anesaki). Marshall Jones Co., Boston

New Golden Bough (A New Abridgement of the Classic Work), The. Sir James George Frazer. Archer Books, New York

Origin of Man and his Superstitions, The. Carveth Read. University Press, Cambridge, England

Panorama of Magic. Milbourne Christopher. Dover Publications, Inc., New York

Playing Cards. W. Gurney Benham. Spring Books, London, England

Teachings of the Magi, The. R. C. Zaehner. Allen and Unwin, London, England

Unmasking of Robert-Houdin, The. Harry Houdini. George Routledge and Sons, Ltd., London, England

Western Response to Zoroaster, The. Jacques Duchesne-Guillemin. Clarendon Press, Oxford, England

Witchcraft, Magic and Alchemy. Grillot de Givry. Bonanza Books, New York

Zoroaster: Politician or Witch-Doctor? Walter Bruno Hermann Henning. Oxford University Press, London, England

Selected Biographies of Famous Magicians

Amazing World of Kreskin, The. Kreskin. Avon Books, New York

Cardano the Gambling Scholar. Oystein Ore. Dover Publications, Inc., New York

Dai Vernon Book of Magic, The. Lewis Ganson, Harry Stanley. Unique Magic Studio, London, England

"Derek Dingle" from Genii magazine, Volume 39, Number 8. William Larsen, Jr., Los Angeles

Dunninger's Secrets. Dunninger, as told to Walter Gibson. Lyle Stuart, Inc., Secaucus

"Glenn Falkenstein" from Genii magazine, Volume 39, Number 1. William Larsen, Jr., Los Angeles

Herrmann the Magician. H. J. Burlingame. Laid and Lee, Chicago

Houdini. Harold Kellock. Harcourt, Brace and Co., New York

Houdini on Magic. Edited by Walter B. Gibson and Morris N. Young. Dover Publications, Inc., New York

Houdini, the Man who Walked through Walls. William Lindsay Gresham. Manor Books, Inc., New York

Houdini, the Untold Story. Milbourne Christopher. Simon and Schuster, Inc. (Pocket Book Division), New York

It Takes all Kinds. Maurice Zolotow. Random House, Inc., New York

"Jimmy Grippo" from Genii magazine, Volume 39, Number 5. William Larsen, Jr., Los Angeles

Malini and his Magic. Dai Vernon. The Supreme Magic Co., Bideford, Devon, England

Memoirs of Robert-Houdin. Jean Éugene Robert-Houdin. Chapman and Hall, London, England

"Merlin of Legend" by Fred Keating. Sphinx magazine. John Mulholland, New York

"Mr. Electric"—Marvyn and Carol Roy from Genii magazine, Volume 38, Number 6. William Larsen, Jr., Los Angeles

My Life of Magic. Howard Thurston. Dorrance and Co., Philadelphia

Other Mr. Churchill: A Lifetime of Shooting and Murder, The. Macdonald Hastings. G. G. Harrap, London, England

White Magic. Jasper Maskelyne. Stanley Paul and Co., Ltd., London, England

The Performance of Magic

Blackstone's Secrets of Magic. Harry Blackstone. A. L. Burt Co., New York and Chicago

Book of Secrets: Miracles, Ancient and Modern, The. Walter Brown Gibson. Personal Arts Co., Scranton

Cyclopedia of Magic. Henry Hay, editor. David McKay Co., New York

Dunninger's Complete Encyclopedia of Magic. Joseph Dunninger. Bonanza Books, New York

Expert at the Card Table, The. S. W. Erdnase. Wehman Bros., New York

Handbook of Magic. Marvin Kaye. Stein and Day, New York

Houdini's Escapes and Magic. Walter B. Gibson. Funk and Wagnalls, New York

Illustrated Magic. Ottokar Fischer. Macmillan Publishing Co., New York

Magic. David H. Charney. Strawberry Hill Publishing Co., New York

Magic. Barrows Mussey. A. S. Barnes Publishing Co., Cranbury

Magic and Showmanship (A Handbook for Conjurers). Henning Nelms. Dover Publications, Inc., New York

Magic of Uri Geller, The. The Amazing Randi. Ballantine Books, New York

Magic: Stage Illusions and Scientific Discoveries Including Trick Photography. Albert A. Hopkins. Martinke and Co., Inc., New York

Modern Magic. Professor Hoffman (Angelo John Lewis). George Routledge and Sons, London, England

Our Magic. Nevil Maskelyne and David Devant. E. P. Dutton and Co., New York

Popular Entertainments through the Ages. Samuel McKechnie. S. Low, Marston and Co., Ltd., London, England

Professional Magic for Amateurs. Walter B. Gibson. Dover Publications, Inc., New York

Scarne on Cards. John Scarne. Crown Publishers, New York

Secrets of Conjuring and Magic, The. Jean Éugene Robert-Houdin. E. P. Dutton and Co., New York

Secrets of Houdini, The. J. C. Cannell. Dover Publications, Inc., New York

Secrets of Modern Conjuring. Horace and Albert Walker. E. P. Dutton and Co., New York

Sleight of Hand. Edwin Sachs. Martinke and Co., New York

Theatre: Three Thousand Years of Drama, Acting and Stagecraft, The. Sheldon Cheney. Tudor Publishing Co., New York

General Reference

An Etymological Dictionary of the English Language. Walter William Skeat. Clarendon Press, Oxford, England

Encyclopedia Britannica. William Benton, Publisher. Tokyo, Manila, Chicago, London, Toronto, Geneva, Sydney

Encyclopedia of Religion and Ethics. James Hastings, editor. Charles Scribners Sons, New York

Origins—A Short Etymological Dictionary of Modern English. Eric Partridge. Routledge and Paul, London, England

The Holy Bible. Translated from the Latin Vulgate, Douay version. Bible House, New York

The Oxford English Dictionary. James A. H. Murray, Henry Bradley, W. A. Craigie, C. T. Onions. Clarendon Press, Oxford, England

INDEX

We would like to thank the following individuals and organizations for their help: the producers of the television show Magic at the Roxy; Richard Salwak, Citrus College, Pasadena, California; Lou Reda, Manager for Kreskin; Elizabeth Fargis, An Evening Dinner Theater, Elmsford, New York; Eastcoast Crane, Inc., Neptune, New Jersey; Bob Leonard, Young President's Organization, New Jersey Chapter; Publicity Department, MGM Grand Hotel, Las Vegas, Nevada; Angela Ferrante, Adelphi University, Garden City, New York; Paul Jacobs, St. John's University, Queens Campus, Jamaica, New York; Gene Bannon, Jersey City State College, Jersey City, New Jersey; Twyla Duncan, Manager for Doug Henning; Walter Heun, E. Leitz Inc.; with special appreciation for the help and editorial guidance of Tony Spina and Irv Tannen of Louis Tannen, Inc., The World's Largest Mail Order Magic Supplier, 1540 Broadway, New York 10036.

Assisting in the production of this book were: Thom Augusta, Elizabeth Henley, Christopher Jones, Patricia Lee, Ruth Forst Michel, Nancy Naglin, Sylvia Sherwin, and Leslie Strong.

Special thanks for their tireless advance and post-operations work: Barnet Friedman and Betty Friedman.

The display faces for this book are Novel Gothic and Futura Neon Outline, set at Latent Lettering Co., Inc. The text faces are Century Expanded and Spartan Bold, set at Tree Communications, Inc. The text paper is 105 gsm., Satin Coated; the tinted paper is 128 gsm., Satsuki. Color separations, halftones, printing, and binding were done by Dai Nippon Printing Co., Ltd., Tokyo, Japan.

Photographer's note: The photographs for this book were taken with Leica M4, M5, and Leicaflex SL MOT cameras. A motor drive was used for photographing fast sequence tricks and illusions. The lenses used were Leitz 35mm, 50mm, and 90mm Summicron f2.0, and 28mm, 135mm, and 180mm Elmarit f2.8. A Leitz 50mm Noctilux f1.2 was used when the lighting was very poor. In most cases existing light was used with Kodak High Speed Ektachrome Tungsten film for color and Kodak Tri-X or 2475 Recording film for black and white. In a few cases electronic flash, bounced off an umbrella, was used for supplemental lighting. These, as well as daylight situations, were shot on Kodachrome 25 and processed by Eastman Kodak Processing Laboratory, Fairlawn, New Jersey. The Ektachrome film was processed by Berkey K + L Custom Services in New York City. The black and white film was processed and printed by Portogallo and Galate, New York City. All the photographs in this book were taken during actual performances; no special effects were used.